Motorbooks International

MUSCLE CAR COLOR HISTORY

CHARGER, ROAD RUNNER & SUPER BEE

Paul A. Herd and Mike Mueller

First published in 1994 by Motorbooks International Publishers & Wholesalers, PO Box 2, 729 Prospect Avenue, Osceola, WI 54020 USA

Motorbooks International books are also available at discounts in bulk quantity for industrial or sales-promotional use. For details write to Special Sales Manager at the Publisher's address

Library of Congress Cataloging-in-Publication Data

Herd, Paul A.
    Charger, Road Runner & Super Bee/
    Paul A. Herd, Mike Mueller.
        p. cm. — (Motorbooks International
        muscle car color history)
    ISBN 0-87938-844-7
    1. Dodge Charger automobile—History.
2. Road Runner automobile—History. 3.
Super Bee automobile—History. 4. Muscle
cars—United States—History. I. Mueller,
Mike. II. Title. III. Title: Charger, Road
Runner, and Super Bee. IV. Series.
    TL215.D627H47   1994
    629.222'2—dc20   93-34444

Printed and bound in Hong Kong

On the front cover: Plymouth's winged warrior, the 1970 Superbird, so dominated NASCAR racing that the rules was rewritten to exclude it. This fine example belongs to Bill and Barbara Jacobsen, Silver Dollar Classic Cars, Odessa, Florida.

On the frontispiece: In case you were wondering what was under the hood...

On the title page: Plymouth's GTX was an upscale muscle car compared to its Road Runner sibling. This 1969 version belongs to Greg Rager of Lakeland, Florida.

On the back cover: A very rare Hemi-powered, Special Edition-equipped Charger R/T belonging to Steve Siegel of Lakeland, Florida.

Contents

Acknowledgments

This book would not have been possible without a lengthy list of individuals. Thanks to Tom Houston, Chrysler Public Relations, who helped me obtain an interview with Bill Brownlie; Brandt Rosenbusch, Chrysler History collection, who supplied the factory and race car photos; Vicki Bohlsen, Special Events; Grace Ann Wireman; and K. C. Winston.

A special thanks to those who let us photograph their cars: Mike Russo; Ron Slobe; Roger and Janet Dunkleman; Tony George; Bill and Barbara Jacobson of Silver Dollar Classic Cars; Floyd Garrett; Greg Rager; Stuart Echolls; Steve Siegel; Mike Hatch; Ed Naszcynrec; Marvin and Joan Hughes; Robert Yapell; and John Robbins.

Also a special thanks to Michael Dregni of Motorbooks, who believed in this project, and to both of our families.

But if there is one individual who made this book possible it is Bill Brownlie, whom I had the great pleasure of interviewing. Brownlie added great insight to this book, and without him there would be no Dodge Charger, at least not as we know it. I regret that due to health problems Gordon Cherry and Jack Smith, the founding fathers of the Road Runner, could not be interviewed. Our thoughts are with their families.

Also a thank you for Richard Petty, who, at the time of this writing, was on his last season circling the tracks of NASCAR (somehow racing will never be the same). Like all great athletes, his number (43) was retired with him. With his Petty Blue Plymouth, he sold more Plymouth Road Runners and GTXs than any ad campaign. It is to him this book is dedicated.

Birth and Death of The Muscle Car

High. Performance. Individually, each word means little. But when joined together, they became one of the best automotive selling tools of all time. High-performance vehicles grew out of the factories' need to improve their racing machines. Every manufacturer wanted to be number one. Every manufacturer wanted its latest model to roll into the winner's circle—whether that winner's circle was on the two-lane drag strips of southern California or on a high-banked NASCAR (National Association for Stock Car Automobile Racing) track. Racing rules required that factories build a certain number of units of a particular engine for public use before that engine could qualify for racing. This homologation rule gave birth to limited, over-the-counter or special-order packages such as Chevrolet's 1955 Super Turbo-Fire 195hp 265ci V-8 or the popular 426 Max Wedge/Ramcharger package from Chrysler in 1964.

The public appetite for high-performance grew strong in the late 1950s and early 1960s. In 1962 Chevrolet introduced the first sport package on its full-sized Impala. Although the Super Sport package was mostly a trim option and came standard with the lowly six-cylinder powerplant, it laid the foundation for things to come. With sales totals of nearly 100,000 units, the Super Sport showed that Americans wanted a performance-image car. And because most SSs were optioned with the V-8 engine, the car also showed that American drivers wanted performance to match looks.

Other auto makers sought to gain some of the performance and youth market Chevrolet's Super Sport was tapping. Ford was fully involved with the Mustang, but Lee Iacocca did not initially see the Mustang as a performance model. Ford was committed to performance, but planned to base it on their full-sized models. In the GM camp, Pontiac had, by 1964, developed a strong performance image with their full-sized Super Duty and tri-powered Catalina and Bonneville, but few young drivers wanted a high-performance "family" car. Pontiac's John DeLorean and marketing guru Jim Wangers understood this, and they envisioned a new performance car aimed directly at the youth market.

Wangers, an ad man with the agency then representing Pontiac, believed that America's youth were bored with cars that looked like their parents' automobiles. He felt that young drivers would snap up cars that were designed to appeal to them. By taking a 389ci V-8 engine, adding a hotter camshaft and 421ci high-compression heads, and placing it into a Le Mans body, Pontiac created the first true muscle car, the GTO.

When the GTO's total sales topped 32,000 in the first year, Detroit's other manufacturers scrambled to develop competing models. Chevrolet was one of the first up, creating the 1965 Chevelle Super Sport by installing its new 396ci Turbo Jet into the frame rails of the mid-sized Chevelle.

In 1966 both Chrysler and Ford each offered a muscle car to tempt the public. Ford borrowed Pontiac's idea and installed a hopped-up big-car engine (in this case a 390ci V-8) into the engine bay of the Fairlane coupe and convertible and called it the Fairlane GT (or GTA with the automatic transmission). Chrysler was putting the final touches on the street version of the 426 Hemi, an engine that had taken all racing honors the year before. Their Dodge division was also getting ready to introduce the Charger. Chrysler would fully enter the muscle marketplace in 1967 with planned introductions of the Plymouth GTX and the Dodge Coronet R/T, both aimed straight at the GTO.

By 1968 all US manufacturers, even staid American Motors, had at least one high-performance image car. Chrysler added to its muscle car line-up, creating two models that would ensure its place in the annals of automotive history: the sleek, racy Dodge

Offered from 1966-1971, there was no other engine like the 426 Hemi. Shown here is a 1968 version in a Road Runner.

Charger and the budget hot rod Road Runner. Chrysler would also up the ante by offering the 440 six-pack—the only multi-carbureted engine available for a mid-sized car.

By the end of the decade, however, big brother, in the form of the EPA, was flexing his muscles. Assisting him

in driving the final few nails into the muscle car's coffin were environmental activists and soaring insurance rates.

Many regard 1970 as the pinnacle year for high-performance with all manufacturers making one final attempt to become the king of the muscle cars. General Motors made mega-cube big blocks available in all of its intermediates. Chevrolet released the 454ci 450hp V-8 in the Chevelle; Pontiac the 455ci 360hp V-8 for the GTO; and Buick the ultra GSX and its 345hp

Stage I 455ci V-8. Ford introduced the 429ci V-8 in Cobra Jet and Super Cobra Jet forms (the latter was rated at 375hp). Chrysler was the only manufacturer who remained confident of its performance potential; it only added the 440 six-pack as an option across the board for its mid-sized muscle cars.

Nineteen seventy-one further weakened the survivors of the war that raged against the muscle car. All manufacturers saw a fall in sales and performance (though the 426 Hemi retained 1970's rating). The battle cry was changing. No longer did the masses beg for a big-block, full-on charger with steel twisting torque; the public's interest was now in miles-per-gallon not miles-per-hour. By 1972 the battle was over. Gone were the Hemis, the over 400hp powerplants, and the multi carburetors. Pontiac made one last effort with the release of the 455 Super Duty V-8 option for the GTO and the Trans Am in 1973 and 1974. But for the most part, the muscle car war had come to an end.

The battle of the muscle car was a long and hard fought one. Today, the models remain like fallen soldiers, with their names etched forever in a wall of memories.

Dodge muscle cars were grouped together in 1968 as part of the Scat Pack. The Charger R/T was leader of the pack. Chrysler

9

Chapter 1

1966–1967

The Rebellion Begins

In the hot Michigan summer of 1962, the Dodge division was offered the chance to share the platform design of Plymouth's Barracuda, which would have been based on its small Lancer model. But Dodge marketing declined for two reasons. First, Dodge had not had much luck in sharing ideas with Plymouth. Most noticeable were the Lancer, which it shared with Plymouth's Valiant, and the ill-fated Seneca model, which it shared with the Plymouth Belvedere. The Seneca model was deleted in 1962, and the Lancer was scheduled to be eliminated in 1963. Second, Dodge had decided to design a model for Chrysler's turbine engine.

Dodge hoped to create a new image by hiring new personnel. They hired Bill Brownlie as the director of design. Brownlie, a young designer both in age and at heart, loved cars. He lived, ate, and dreamed cars. "It wasn't just something I put on when I came to work," he said. Knowing all great designs start with an idea, Dodge also hired Burt Bouwkamp as product planning manager. Bouwkamp, a weekend motorcycle racer, also did not see cars as just work.

Changes to the 1967 Charger were few. Styled wheels were a new option.

Only a small fender ID plate provides a clue to what's powering this Plymouth.

Brownlie and his staff had not rejected a Barracuda-style fastback design for Dodge, but they opted for a larger sized car. Fastback styling was nothing new—Ford was working on one for the Mustang, and Chevrolet had developed one for the Corvair. But Brownlie and his staff would be the first to graft it onto a larger body.

This fastback body style, as yet unnamed, was being groomed to receive Chrysler's much hyped turbine engine. Elwood P. Engel had created the turbine show car and had stated that, "it was a car of today rather than a futuristic dream car." The show car was the final step in the turbine's development before it was placed in production as a limited-edition model. Dodge planned to measure public reaction by giving a selected number of drivers from around the country a turbine fastback to test. At the last moment, however, the project was scrapped because of a disagreement over which dealers would service the cars. Although the turbine project died, the fastback model it would have propelled survived.

In mid-summer of 1965, Bouwkamp realized that Dodge did not have a model for the lineup at the upcoming auto show. He called in Bill Brownlie and asked him what model they should use. "The Coronet was one of Dodge's best-selling models at the time,"

The Charger II show car featured a sloping roofline and tube grille.

The 1966 Charger looked much like the show car, but hideaway headlamps replaced the tube grille.

Brownlie recalled, "so I suggested a fastback Coronet." Designated as the Charger II (named after the 1963 show car Charger) the model was not a prototype for the 1966 Charger model, as everyone seems to think. It was simply built, remembered Brownlie, "because we did not have an entry in the auto show."

Because of limited time and funds, a fastback was quickly grafted onto a

Coronet two-door hardtop. It was given the customary show car bar grille and full width tail lamps, a feature that was borrowed from the turbine project. The inside was given the most attention with four bucket seats and racy looking instrumentation. Both of these features would find their way into the production model. Since most of the funds were tied up in the styling, a garden

variety 318ci small block V-8 lived beneath the hood.

Public reaction at the show surprised Dodge's marketing executives. When they asked potential customers "Would you buy one if it were built?" the reply was an overwhelming yes.

1966 Charger: The Leader Is Born

The 1966 fastback Charger was introduced at a "Press Gymkhana" for West Coast magazine writers in mid-October 1965. Dodge marketing executives carefully planned this date so that the reviews would show up in the January 1966 issues of various automotive magazines; the same time the Charger would make its public appearance. The marketing executives desired a grand entrance for the Charger, so they bought time for a commercial to air January 1, 1966, during the Rose Bowl Game's half time. While the UCLA and Michigan State players prepared for the second half, actress/model Pam Austin told millions of captivated viewers that "the Dodge Rebellion wants you!" Not only did she introduce the sleek fastback Charger, but also the beginning of the new Dodge Motor division.

The relationship between the Charger II show car and the production model was evident. The swept back roofline that graduated into the deck lid was retained. The backlight, which was flat and literally faced the sky, was a great improvement over the fish bowl type that was used on the Barracuda. The Charger had strong ties to the Coronet, and this was particularly noticeable below the beltline. In fact, the models used the same wheelbase of 117in; and the Charger, with its sloping fastback, was just a fraction longer than the Coronet at 203-1/2in.

A major difference between the show car and the production model was the grille. The flashy show car grille was replaced with a full-width convex one with fine vertical bars and hideaway headlamps. This marked the first use of hideaway headlamps on a Dodge model. When the headlamp switch was turned on, the headlamps rotated into

The sleek, fastback styling made the first-generation Charger seem more aerodynamic than it was.

The Charger's interior came with standard bucket seats and full instrumentation.

view. An override switch, which allowed the headlamps to rotate into view but not be turned on, was also placed on the instrument panel. This was a practical feature especially for those cars driven in cold weather climates where the doors might freeze shut, a problem that Chevrolet had encountered with the 1963 Corvette's hidden headlamps. To give the grille an uncluttered look, the turn signal lamps were also placed behind the slated grille located on the outboard sides.

The Dodge name was spelled out in the center of the hood's front edge. A Dodge delta emblem was positioned in the grille's center, and the Charger script emblem was placed on the arched C-pillars along with a medallion, commonly known as the Charger emblem. The chirography of the Charger script shows Brownlie's influence. "I love to see script writing on a car," he said. "I would work at home trying to get it just right." The Charger name was also spelled out across the full width taillamps.

When viewed from the rear, there was the slight look of tail fins where the quarter panels meet the deck lid;

another differing feature between the Charger and Coronet. Other differences included more pronounced body side design lines with simulated air vents in front of the rounded rear wheelwell openings (Coronet's wore half skirt wheelwells). The rounded opening eased the fitting of wider racing tires.

Inside, the Charger's interior was rich and elegant—ads compared it to a luxury car. Nearly everything was standard. There was thick, pile door-to-door carpeting and fully foam-padded bucket seats front and rear (another feature taken from the show car). The upper portions of the door and quarter trim panels were molded plastic in the

same color as the interior and trimmed with brushed aluminum trim plates. Carpeting, which matched that on the floor, covered the lower portion of the panel.

The bucket seat covers were done in coachman grain embossed with thin vertical pleating. The rear seat design was borrowed from the Barracuda, and each seatback could be folded down individually. The seatbacks were carpeted as was the security panel that separated the interior compartment from the trunk area. This panel could also be folded down. When the security panel and both rear seatbacks were folded down, drivers had a total cargo space of 4ftx7-1/2ft. Five interior colors were available: blue, Saddle Tan, red, white, and gold/black.

The instrument panel was one of the Charger's strongest features. It was also one of the most complete systems

offered that year by any US manufacturer. The basic design consisted of four large, round pods. At the far left were alternator and fuel level gauges. Just to the left of the steering column was what would become a Charger trademark: 150mph speedometer. To the steering column's right was a 6000rpm tachometer. Most car makers offered an optional tachometer, but Dodge made it standard on the sporty Charger. Finishing up the gauges at the far right was a combination temperature and oil pressure gauge. Below the bright trimmed gauges and to the left were the controls for headlamp door override, headlamps, wipers, and emergency flashers; to the right were the hood release, ignition, and cigarette lighter.

Heater and air conditioning controls were located in the center of the instrument panel just above the option-

Folding rear bucket seats were an idea borrowed from the Plymouth Barracuda.

al radio. A checkered, matte black finishing plate was used over the radio and heater area. This same pattern was carried over to the glovebox door with bright trim tracing the outlines.

Another standard item on the Charger, which was usually an extra cost item in other models, was a three spoke simulated wood rimmed steering wheel. No other steering wheel was available. When either the automatic transmission or four speed manual was ordered, a full length console was also standard. This meant that no 1966 Chargers were built with automatic on the column. Options that owners could add to dress up their Chargers included padded sun visors, remote control left-hand door mirror, air conditioning,

17

Here, laid out in all its glory, is the 425hp king of the street: the 426 Hemi.

power brakes, power steering, power windows, and a host of performance options.

Standard power for the Charger came from a 318ci V-8 making 230hp at 4400rpm and 340lbs-ft of torque at 2400rpm. The 318ci powerplant was the only engine available with the standard transmission, which was a three-speed, column-shifted manual. A 361ci two-barrel V-8 rated at 265hp was optional. Also optional was a big block 383ci four-barrel V-8 producing 325hp at 4800rpm and 425lbs-ft of torque at

2800rpm. This last engine was the best performer for the daily driver. When this engine was ordered, emblems that read "383 Four Barrel" were placed on the front fenders just behind the wheel-well openings.

Available as the top performance option was the 426 Hemi, basically a detuned version of the racing engine introduced in 1965. Compression was reduced and the aluminum cylinder heads were replaced with cast iron units. This mammoth engine was not a true production option. It was available only as a special order.

The 426 Hemi pumped out 425hp at 5000rpm with 490lbs-ft of tire melting torque coming on at 4000rpm. The

Hemi was fed by two Carter AFB four-barrels hiding under a large chrome air cleaner. In an ad, Dodge called the Hemi Charger the "Beauty and the Beast. Looks like a pampered thoroughbred but comes on like Genghis Khan." When the Hemi was ordered, the heavy-duty Rallye suspension was added consisting of a nearly 1in thick front sway bar and large diameter torsion bars rated at 118sq-in. In the back was a 9-3/4in Dana 60 rear axle (with the four-speed manual) or 8-3/4in with Sure-Grip differential (with the automatic transmission).

Standard tires were 7.35x14in blackwalls. Hemi-equipped cars were shod with 7.75x14in Good Year Blue

Win a 426 Hemi!

In 1966 the Plymouth lineup lacked a muscle car (the GTX was still in the works). However, it offered muscle in the form of the 426 Hemi for its restyled Belvedere model. Like the Charger, the Hemi Belvedere included a heavy-duty suspension with police-model brakes, though this option could be had on any Belvedere—even a four-door with dog-dish style hubcaps. Only a small emblem on the front fenders alerted drivers

continued on next page

Although Plymouth lacked a true muscle car model, they offered the 426 Hemi in all Belvederes like this Satellite.

Rear view of a Hemi-equipped 1966 Plymouth Satellite.

If you had known it would take Jim Hurtubise 3 hours, 49 minutes, and 2 seconds to win the 1966 Atlanta 500, this Hemi powerplant installed in any Belvedere could have been yours for free.

to what lurked beneath this car's hood. The high-class Satellites, most of which were ordered with the 426 Hemi, also included a stand-up hood ornament that read "426 Hemi."

Plymouth ran a giveaway contest in 1966 and the prize was a 426 Hemi-powered Belvedere two-door hardtop Satellite. The prize car included a radio, automatic transmission, power steering and brakes, knock off hub wheel covers, bucket seats, and console. To enter, contestants had to guess the running time of the Atlanta 500, along with the average winning speed. In the case

of a tie, the two winners had to also identify the number of laps the winning driver led.

Although history has lost the outcome of Plymouth's contest, the result of the oval contest is in the record books. Jim Hurtubise took the checkered flag driving a 1966 Plymouth. His time was 3 hours, 49 minutes, 2 seconds, with an average speed of 131.247mph. He was race leader for 131 of the 334 laps.

streaks. Cars with air conditioning (not available with the Hemi) used 7.75x15in blackwall tires. Deluxe full wheel covers were standard and mag-style covers were optional.

Hot Rod magazine remarked "with its slippery shape we wouldn't rule out the sight of a Dodge Charger or two making it around some of the NASCAR banked ovals." Yet the design was not as sleek as it looked; when running at high speeds, the tail would begin to drift. Dodge sent a 3/8-scale model of the Charger to Kansas State University for wind tunnel testing. The tests showed that Dodge could solve their problem by adding a rear spoiler.

At the Firecracker 400 on July 4, 1966, Sam McQuagg showed up with a rear lip spoiler bolted to the rear deck of his Charger stock car. The officials deemed it legal because Dodge offered it as an option to the public. McQuagg went on to win the race—a first for him and the Dodge Charger.

1967: More Muscle Is Added

In the spring of 1966, word leaked back to Highland Park that Pontiac was planning to phase out the 389ci engine used in the GTO and replace it with a 400ci powerplant. It was rumored that horsepower might be around 370 with a single four barrel. The rumors proved to be slightly exaggerated as the top engine managed only 360hp.

In the late 1960s, cubic inches and horsepower sold cars, and if you had more than the other guys then it was all the better. Chrysler engineers knew this. To combat against the 400ci General Motors powerplants, they had to have something bigger and more powerful. The decision was made to use the big displacement 440ci V-8 that had been introduced as a Chrysler option in 1966. In standard form with a four-barrel carburetor, the 440 was rated at 350hp at 4400rpm. Because of the rumors of the 370hp GTO engine, however, Chrysler wanted to pass that mark. Besides, if the standard passenger car rating was retained the engine would be regarded as nothing but "a big-car engine."

One of the 440's weak points was its cylinder head design which produced a low power peak and had restrictive ports. To correct this, special heads were cast featuring larger 1.76in diameter exhaust valves and intake ports enlarged a full 10 percent over the standard units. Stiffer valve springs were fitted to better control valve movement. Bench flow tests found these heads to flow 90 percent of the volume flowed by the heads used on the 426 Max Wedge/Ramcharger racing heads.

Further modifications included a camshaft with more duration (268 degrees intake and 260 degrees exhaust) and greater overlap (46 degree) and a large Carter AFB carburetor with mechanical secondaries. Engines destined for California used a smaller Carter carb with vacuum operated secondaries. A free-flowing dual exhaust system exiting through 2-1/2in diameter tailpipes was also part of the package.

When run on the dynamometer, the engine registered a peak horsepower of 375 at 4600rpm and 480lbs-ft of torque at 3200rpm. This high-performance 440 was made available for Dodge and Plymouth mid-sized models (in a Dodge, it would be called 440 Magnum; in the Plymouth it was known as a 440 Super Commando). It would also become the base powerplant for Chrysler's two newest muscle cars: the Coronet R/T and the Plymouth GTX.

1967 Charger: Dodge's White Stallion

Changes were few for the fastback Dodge's second year. Except for the addition of front fender turn indicators and an optional vinyl roof in either black or white, the exterior was unchanged. Front and rear bucket seats remained standard, but they used a new pattern of vertical pleating with a medallion placed in the center of each seatback. The console was now an extra cost item with either an automatic or four-speed manual gearbox. It was shorter than the one used in 1966 and did not extend into the rear seat area. The wood rim steering wheel was now optional and a three-spoke, color-keyed, plastic rim steering wheel with a partial horn ring was made standard.

Mechanical changes included a dual system brake master cylinder, collapsible steering column, and a day/night inside mirror with a double balljoint safety mount. All of these items were mandatory safety equip-

ment required by federal regulations. The base 318ci V-8 was redesigned and was about 60lb lighter due to the furan cone casting process. The cylinder heads also used a wedge-type combustion chamber instead of 1966's polysphere, yet the horsepower rating remained the same. The 361ci two-barrel option was replaced by a 383ci two-barrel version rated at 270hp at 4400rpm. The 383ci four-barrel returned unchanged, and the Hemi became a regular production option. In between was the 375hp 440 Magnum V-8 which cut heavily into Hemi sales.

1967 Coronet R/T: Dodge's Other Muscle Car

The 1966 Charger was not intended to be a true muscle car. Instead, Dodge marketing aimed it at the specialty car market then populated by such vehicles as the Thunderbird, Riviera, and Toronado. As Bouwkamp claimed at the time, "The coming thing in design is the intermediate-sized specialty car." And Dodge at the time did not truly consider the Charger a super car. Bouwkamp saw a revamped Coronet 500 as the Dodge counterpart to the successful GTO and christened the new car the Coronet R/T (R/T standing for Road and Track). He hailed it as "a dual purpose machine," at home on the racetrack or the shaded streets of a small town. The Coronet R/T was available as either a two-door hardtop or a convertible.

To give the model a distinctive look, Dodge used a grille that simulated the look of the Charger with its headlamps exposed. A large red-and-black R/T emblem was placed on the far left-hand side of the grille. This nameplate was also placed on the rear quarter panels on the beltline just in front of the rear wheelwell openings. An insert trim panel that duplicated the grille texture was placed on the rear edge of the deck lid and over the taillamps. An R/T nameplate was positioned on the passenger side of the deck lid. At the time, simulated hood scoops were the "in" thing to have on a muscle car (the GTO and the Chevelle SS 396 had them), so

Next page
The Coronet R/T was Dodge's answer to the Pontiac GTO.

A Charger-like grille highlighted the 1967 Coronet.

The taillamp panel on the mid-sized Dodge matched the grille's pattern.

simulated louvers were placed at the rear edge of the Coronet R/T's hood.

Inside was the Coronet 500's interior trim of fully padded, foam front bucket seats done in a design and grain that was similar to the Charger's. The R/T's rear seat was a conventional bench design. The most noticeable thing about the instrument panel was the addition of a 150mph speedometer housed in a long rectangular pod just in front of the driver. To the speedometer's left was the alternator and fuel level gauges, and to the right were a water temperature gauge and a clock. An oil pressure warning lamp was positioned within the speedometer housing. The crosshatch design texture used in the Charger was carried over into the R/T on the glovebox door and trim panel around the radio.

To ensure the "track" portion of the R/T name was satisfied, the standard power for this model was the all new 440 Magnum with the Hemi being the only optional powerplant. The standard gearbox was the Torque Flight heavy-duty automatic with a column-mounted

shift lever. A console, which placed the shifter lever on the floor was optional at extra cost. A four-speed manual transmission was a no-cost option. A fold-down center armrest was also optional but only with an automatic on the column. Interior trim was available in blue, black, copper, red, gold/black, or white/black. The latter two colors used a black carpet and instrument panel with a black headliner in the hardtop models.

1967 GTX: Plymouth's Answer to the GTO

Plymouth's Chief Product Planning Manager Jack L. Smith realized that Plymouth needed a new image. The company's models had always been thought of as the spinster schoolteacher's car. Dodge's reincarnation had already begun, and Smith was not going to let Plymouth fall by the wayside. In previous years, a family sedan might have been a hot-selling model, but the GTO and Mustang opened up new market areas. Plymouth's Barracuda was aimed at the Mustang, but

The Coronet R/T's interior looked similar to the Charger's. Front bucket seats were the only seating arrangement available.

the company had no model to lure away GTO buyers.

Smith knew that model names with three letters or numbers were popular. One day at his desk he began jotting down names on a yellow legal pad. He wrote down the letters GT and began going through the alphabet. GTA? No, Ford was using that on automatic equipped Fairlane GTs. GTS? Again no; Dodge was using that name on the Dart. Nearly running out of letter he came across the letter "X." GTX. It

Rated at 375hp, the 440 Magnum was the most powerful standard engine available from any of Detroit's big three.

sounded good, and the first true Plymouth muscle car was born.

Smith ordered up Studio Chief Richard McAdams and they discussed the idea in detail. McAdams suggested that they use the Satellite as a base. This model was well trimmed and offered both a two-door hardtop and convertible as the most popular models.

Smith agreed. McAdams wanted the GTX "to have all the customary performance car accessories but to improve on them." He and his staff added twin hood scoops on the hood. Although they were not functional, they looked more real than any other models offered that year. Due to the high cost of casting the hood scoops, the GTX had to use the stan-

Driving under an open blue sky in a Hemi-powered ragtop—that was true happiness.

dard Satellite grille. Milt Antonick was responsible for the use of the pit stop-style gas cap on the driver's side rear quarter—a performance-look item he had also used on the 1967 Barracuda

27

The Hemi was also optional in the Plymouth convertible. Very few were built, however.

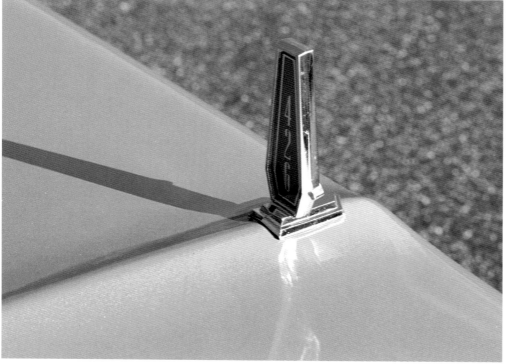

Plymouth was spelled out across the hood's front edge, and a stand-up hood ornament carried the engine call-out. Belvedere nameplates were carried high on the forward section of the front fenders, and just below them was the GTX emblem. The GTX name was also placed on the rear edge of the deck lid on the passenger side.

Inside, no 1967 muscle car wore a richer looking interior than the GTX. "The GTX interior oozes luxury," stated a 1967 Belvedere sales brochure. Thick

A stand-up hood ornament let onlookers know what was underfoot.

Next page
Plymouth's first true muscle car was the GTX. Note the race-style gas cap on the side.

The GTX featured aggressive-looking, non-functional hood scoops as part of its performance package.

door-to-door carpeting and fully padded, foam bucket seats done in deeply embossed vinyl were standard. A large, square 150mph speedometer dominated the instrument panel. To the speedometer's left were small rectangular gauges for the engine temperature and the fuel level; below them were the light and wiper controls. On the speedometer's right were the alternator and oil pressure gauges. Just below them were controls for the heater and air conditioning. On the instrument panel's lower portion was the toggle switch for the four-way flashers, the ignition switch, and the cigarette

lighter. Convertible models also had a power top button located there.

When air conditioning was ordered (available only with the 440ci V-8) the center vents were located in the middle of the instrument panel directly above the optional radio. A crosshatch, black accented trim plate was placed over the glovebox door, which also sported the GTX name.

The standard steering wheel was a three-spoke with a color-keyed plastic rim and a half horn-ring. A three-spoke steering wheel with a simulated walnut rim was optional. A center console was optional with either the standard automatic or the no-cost optional four-speed manual transmission; the console could be optionally fitted with a 6000rpm tachometer. A fold-down, center armrest was optional but could only be ordered if no console was fitted. Also, like

the Coronet R/T, the only optional engine was the 426 Hemi.

Both the GTX and the Coronet were fitted with the police car suspension and brakes as standard equipment. The police suspension included thicker front torsion bars, front anti-sway bar, and staggered rear leaf springs (six full leaves on the right and five full with two half leaves on the left). The staggered rear eliminated wheel hop under hard acceleration. Also standard were 11in diameter drum brakes. This same suspension was also used on Hemi-equipped cars, thus the public came to know it as the "hemi suspension."

Other options available for the GTX included twin racing stripes (in white, black, blue, red, light tan, and medium copper) for the hood and deck lid, power steering, power brakes,

The 1967 GTX's interior was rich and elegant.

headrests, and power front disc brakes. Headrests, shoulder belts for the front seat passengers, and mag-style wheel covers rounded out the options list.

A popular option for all models was the new Road Wheels. These were 14x5-1/2in wheels featuring a five-spoke pattern with black accented insets and bright plated center cap, lug nuts, and outer rim. These wheels came with 7.75x14in red streak tires.

The GTX was nicknamed "the Boss" years before Ford slapped that moniker on a Mustang fastback. And, unlike Ford, the name was not just a

A tachometer was optional in both the R/T and the GTX, but only when the optional console was fitted.

Richard Petty became the king of stock car racing with this car, which took the checkered flag a record twenty-seven times. *Chrysler*

Two Carter AFB *four-barrel carburetors fed the 426 Hemi.*

marketing ploy. The GTX was the Boss because it was nearly unbeatable in both drag racing and on the NASCAR circuit. Richard Petty earned his title "King Richard" by putting his Plymouth blue, number forty-three GTX in the winner's circle a mind-blowing twenty-seven times, including ten consecutive wins. Plymouth's and Petty's strong hold was so tight that Petty finished in the top ten of all but eight races. Coincidence or not, it remains a fact that most GTXs were sold in the week following one of Petty's wins.

In the Plymouth line, the 375hp V-8 was called the 440 Super Commando. It was standard in the GTX.

Chapter 2

1968–1970

Scat Pack and the Rapid Transit System

1968: Dodge's Year of Change

In the fall of 1966, Bill Brownlie walked into Dodge Exterior Design Studios and began work on the 1968 models, which, according to Dodge's two to three year styling cycle, were scheduled for an entirely new look. The basic design of the Coronet was now two years old; a re-skinning occurred in 1966, but it was still the basic 1965 model. The 1966 Coronet lacked the graceful lines of its competitors and appeared dated when compared to GM's restyled bodies. Despite this, the decision was made to save the restyle for the 1968 models.

For 1967 Dodge marketing had abandoned its "join the rebellion" ad scheme for a "road and track" theme. "I wanted the ultimate road and track machine," Brownlie said, "and the Coronet R/T was not that car." Instead, Brownlie wanted to redesign the Charger as something distinctly different from the Coronet. So in addition to restyling the other 1968 models, Brownlie gave his staff of nine another assignment: Design a new Charger "that looked like it could run around the high banks of Daytona but still could be driven on the

Bob Rodger's concept car, the Charger 500, was designed specifically for NASCAR racing.

Seals and an underhood air box directed air through the trapdoor to the carbs on the Plymouth models.

streets." This was the car he had envisioned when he named the fastback Coronet the Charger.

The designers submitted their visions of what the new Charger should look like. Ultimately, it was a young designer named Richard Tighstin who came up with the look that was closest to Brownlie's vision of the perfect car. "It just looked like a Charger," Brownlie said of Tighstin's design. "I could just see it charging down the street." The Charger's new design was a tapered look, narrow at the front and wider toward the rear of the car. "I was a believer in aerodynamics at the time," Brownlie said. "I wanted a shape you could see." When viewed as a profile, the car's wedged shapes really shows. The sheet metal curves upwards at the end creating a built-in rear lip spoiler. As tests showed, a rear spoiler significantly helped in racing. Also, the built-in design would further influence the stock car look that Brownlie wanted.

Up front, the full width grill and hideaway headlamps became an identifying Charger feature, lending the car "that stock car look" of taped-over headlamps, as Brownlie explained it. Due to cost considerations and weight-saving measures, the design was changed, however. The quad headlamps were fixed in place and lightweight plastic doors rose up and back when the driver

If it takes more than a brand-new style to turn you on,

here's more.

Congratulations ... you've got Dodge fever

'68 Dodge Charger. What a great shape to be in.

Tired of all those look-alike shapes around you? The ones that surround you at every traffic light? Why not take a look at Dodge Charger for 1968? Then take a good look at all the goodies that meet you when you open Charger's door. This one's different, inside and out. Outside, you've already seen. Inside, all business. Foam-padded bucket seats to coddle you. Matt-finished instruments with black faces, white numbers and needles. Meant to be read often. Two deep and handy door pockets for all the paraphernalia that usually collects under your feet. A range of four engines to suit your driving needs. (Up to the 440-cubic-inch Magnum V8 in Charger R/T.) Switches that do interesting things, like make the concealed headlights appear on command. In short, a car with everything you need to make you take an interest in cars again. And the price makes Charger doubly easy to take. Low enough to give you a high case of Dodge Fever. Got the idea? Got the Fever? Now stop at your Dodge Dealer's and sign up for the cure. Your very own Charger—right now. It's the only cure for Dodge Fever.

'68 CHARGER

Drive safely. It's also contagious.

Dodge CHRYSLER MOTORS CORPORATION

"Dodge Fever" was the theme of 1968's ad campaign, led by the all new Charger. Chrysler

model used the R/T emblem instead of the medallion.

Not one single piece of sheet metal on the Charger is the same as the Coronet, including the hood. The Charger's hood was wide and flat except for one simulated air vent on each side. These vents not only were decorative but also helped improve the hood's stiffness. Brownlie recalls, however, that he tried to make the vents functional. "I wanted the vents to be open to allow the engine heat to escape," he explained. "But standards were against this because the fear of water leakage into the engine compartment." The simulated vents were also copied on to the front edge of the doors.

Hood-mounted turn indicators were very popular, yet these barely made it to production. As Brownlie recalled, the electrical department felt the lights could not withstand everyday use. "They were afraid that bulbs would burn out every time the hood was slammed," Brownlie said. "I assured them that would not happen, and they finally agreed."

Brownlie could not, however, get approval for his idea of dual flip-top gas caps that would be mounted on the top of each of the muscular rear quarter panels. "I wanted a design that would allow a driver to pull into any service station and fill up, and not worry about what side the filler neck was on," he said. But management questioned the extra cost. Brownlie pleaded his case, but to no avail. This confrontation came near the beginning of production. "If you look closely," Brownlie said, "you will see that all the clay models have dual gas caps."

In fact, it was only Brownlie's insistence that ensured the flip-top gas cap was used at all. The concern was that the cap could freeze over in the winter in the northern states. "I told them," Brownlie said, "that anyone who bought this car would carry an ice pick so they could have this car." Brownlie said the Charger "was for the man who wants to be the first on his block to own it. So he could have a car like no other car on the road." Brownlie finally won over the brass and they agreed to the flip-top gas cap; a feature that has become a Charger trademark.

One of the most unique things about the Charger was the tunneled

driver could manually raise the doors into position. The system was vacuum operated and considerably lighter than the 1966–1967 design.

The Charger script was placed on the grille as was the Charger medallion. Dodge's Road and Track package was also carried over to the Charger's newest model the Charger R/T. This

turned on the headlamp switch. The headlight override switch was eliminated from the instrument panel, but the

The stock car look of the 1968 Charger made it an instant success with buyers and critics alike. Chrysler

rear window design. Except for the Corvette, no other American car was like it. The Charger's bold roofline truly gave it a muscular race car look. *Car and Driver* magazine agreed stating, "the only car close to it is the [1968] Corvette." The magazine gave the top styling honor to the Charger for the reason that the Corvette "has a much easier time attaining the desired sporty image" due to its size. "There was talk about a fastback," Brownlie said, "but the tunnel rear window was what I wanted all along." As in 1967, the Charger script was used on the C-pillars followed by the colored medallion

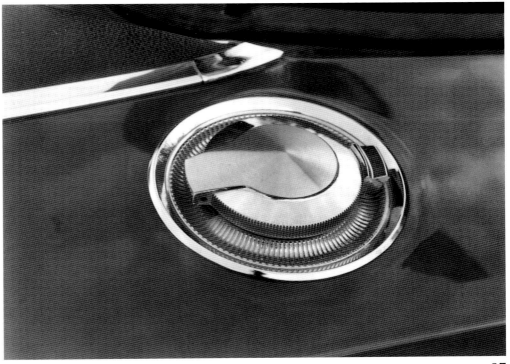

The Charger's flip-top gas cap added to its race car look.

37

Chrysler's winning ways extended to the drag strip as well. The Landy brothers campaigned a pair of Dodges for 1968. Dick (at left) drove the Hemi-powered Charger R/T, and Mike (right) ran the 440 Magnum-equipped Coronet R/T. Chrysler

on base Chargers only. Charger R/T's did not use the medallion on the roof.

At the Charger's rear was a flat-black accented taillamp panel that was slanted inward at the bottom with the top meeting nearly flush with the deck lid's rear edge. Full width taillamps were replaced with two round units on each side with the Charger script lying between. An R/T nameplate followed the Charger script on that model while the Dodge medallion followed the base Charger's script. "Other taillamps seen on clay models were just experiments with different designs," Brownlie said. "I pretty much had decided on the round style."

Brownlie's stock-car-look exterior heavily influenced the interior design studio's final product. The designers carried the race car theme to the instrument panel, which consisted of two large-faced gauges flanked on the right by four smaller gauges. The leftmost gauge was large clock, though a combination clock and tachometer was optional. Next was the 150mph speedometer. To the steering column's left were the four small gauges for fuel level, temperature, oil pressure, and alternator. Customers had complained about the gauge package used in 1966 and 1967 saying the instruments were hard to read in the daytime. For 1968, the gauges were deeply inset in a matte black bezel, which also housed the accessories controls. The bezel eliminated the light reflections that had plagued the earlier models.

Positioned on the instrument panel's far left-hand side was a bright, plat-ed rocker switch for the headlamps. A knurled knob to control the interior level lighting was next to it. Below that was a red lens for the brake warning lamp and another bright rocker switch for the emergency flashers. Below the rightmost two small gauges were the controls for the wipers and a push button for the washers.

A fresh air hot water heater and defroster were standard on both Charger models and the push-pull controls were located high in the center of the instrument panel, just above the optional radio. If air conditioning was ordered, its controls were integrated with the heater. The center outlet vent was located below the radio. Below this was an ashtray and lighter. The glovebox door was padded and hinged at the top.

Front bucket seats were still standard, but the rear fold-down bucket seats were replaced by a conventional stationary bench seat. The door panels

were a two-part design: a molded upper section sported a round Charger medallion in the middle, and the lower door panels were fiberboard covered with pleated vinyl. The standard steering wheel was a three-spoke color-keyed unit with partial horn ring. A full horn ring steering wheel and the simulated walnut rim wheel were each optional.

Powerplants and drivetrain were the same as in 1967 except for slight modifications to the 440 and Hemi engines. In the case of the 440, the heads were recast, while the Hemi received hotter spark plugs to cure an oil fouling problem. In both cases the modifications improved the driveability of cars equipped with those engines. The

Charger R/T came standard with the 375hp 440 Magnum with the Hemi listed as the only option. Neither the 440 nor Hemi was available in the base Charger model. The largest engine available for the base model was the 383 four-barrel rated at 330hp.

1968 Coronet: Running with the Pack

With the exception of powerplants and drivetrains, 1968's Coronet R/T was all new. Dodge's newest marketing ploy was the Scat Pack, an elite group of boulevard heavies including the Charger R/T, the Dart GTS, the Coronet, and, later in the model year, the Super Bee. All had twin racing stripes

The 375hp Magnum V-8 supplied standard power for the new Charger R/T. The engine breathed through an "unsliced" (no snorkle) air cleaner.

wrapped around the tail end of the car, prompting Dodge to call them bumble bee stripes. *Car Life* magazine stated, "those cars must really be fast—they almost got past the striper." While most stripes ran the length of the car, Dodge designers shook the industry with ones that ran the width of the car.

The Coronet R/T was still offered as a convertible and the popular two-door hardtop. The new body was placed on a 117in wheelbase; length was 207in from

All 1968 B-bodys were restyled including the Coronet R/T. A styled hood sporting simulated air vents was again part of the package. Chrysler

the tip of the bow to the tip of the stern (which was about 4in longer than in 1967). But because the new design was narrower by 7in than the previous model, it looked even longer. The car also sat lower on its haunches than in 1967, giving it a more aggressive stance.

Body lines were rounder and contour lines less pronounced than in 1967. And even though the Charger and Coronet share not one single piece of sheet metal, there is still a strong family resemblance.

The Coronet's grille was set deeply into the nose and used a fine cross-hatch pattern; this design was also carried over to the headlamp bezels. Both the grille and the headlamp bezels were accented in black. A large red-and-black R/T nameplate was placed on the driver's side of the grille. These nameplates were also used on the front fenders and the rear taillamp panel, which was accented by a concave matte black trim panel. The Dodge name was spelled out beneath this trim plate.

Simulated hood vents were placed along the sides of a raised dome in the center of the hood. Inside, the Coronet

R/T was done in a deluxe all vinyl interior with front bucket seats. The door panels were one-piece fiberboard covered with heavily sculptured vinyl. The upper portions of the door were painted and held a rectangular shaped Coronet R/T nameplate with black background and red lettering. Standard instrumentation included a 150mph speedometer in the center flanked by an alternator and fuel gauges on the left and a temperature gauge on the right. Just to the right of the temperature gauge was an optional clock or tachometer; unlike the Charger they could not be ordered as a unit. If drivers wanted a true oil pressure gauge, they had to order the optional Rallye gauge package, which matched the Charger instrumentation, and included a combination clock and tachometer as standard. A power top was standard on the convertible and a bright rocker switch was placed next to the wiper controls on both types of instrumentation.

1968 Super Bee: Striped not Stripped

By the spring of 1967, news that Plymouth was working on a low-budget performance car called the Road Runner had filtered its way down to Dodge. But Dodge decided not to offer a companion model at the beginning of

production. Instead, they wanted to focus on the new Charger, which outsold the Plymouth more than two to one. The company, however, saw that there was a need for a car like the Road Runner, which sold quickly and piled up the orders.

Following the Road Runner formula, Burt Bouwkamp based the Super Bee on the low-ball Coronet 440 two-door pillar sedan. The design was a little higher in trim than the base Coronet line, which was the equivalent of Plymouth's Belvedere. The Super Bee could be called the model that borrowed from all the other models and never gave anything back. It was powered by the 383 Magnum, Dodge's version of the Road Runner's engine. The Super Bee's standard gearbox was a four-speed manual. Like the R/Ts, the Hemi was optional. Also optional was an automatic transmission with either engine. The Super Bee also borrowed the Coronet R/T's domed hood. Inside, it borrowed the Charger's instrumentation but kept the low trim interior with a standard bench seat. Neither bucket seats nor a console was available as an option. Underneath, the body was a standard heavy-duty suspension and big diameter drum brakes.

The grille was the same as that used on the R/T, but the Dodge name

40

was spelled out across it in bright block lettering. Dodge was also spelled out across the taillamp panel. A bumble bee decal was placed on the rear edge of the deck lid. Since this model was inducted into the Scat Pack family, it was given the twin bumble bee stripes with a larger round decal of the Super Bee name and logo (a bumble bee on fat tires wearing a crash helmet and racing goggles).

The Dodge marketing department was known for the grandstanding way it marketed new models. The Super Bee was no exception. First, marketing executives sent fliers to the dealers proclaiming the new model's release. Then they placed a full-page, colored ad of a bright yellow-and-black Super Bee (the colors of a bumble bee) in issues of *Hot Rod, Car and Driver, Super Stock and Drag Racing Illustrated, Motor Trend, Car Life, Road and Track, Popular Hot Rodding, Drag Strip, Auto Racing,* and *Cars,* and 250 college newspapers—just what the prospective buyer would be reading. Although the model did not (for some reason) achieve Road Runner level sales, it provided Dodge an entrance into the budget muscle car market.

Plymouth for 1968: "Beep Beep"

Early in 1967, the phone rang in Plymouth's Product Planning offices. Joe Strum took the call. On the other end of the line was Brock Yates, a journalist from *Car and Driver Magazine.* Yates proposed an idea to Strum: build a stripped-down business coupe stuffed with a 440 Super Commando or Hemi as standard equipment; include front bucket seats but no rear seat. Also, make styled wheel covers or styled wheels standard. The idea sounded somewhat like Carroll Shelby's 1965 GT 350 Mustang. Yet Yates wanted no outside gimmicks, trim, engine ID badges, stripes, or hood scoops. The final catch: sell it all for less than $3,000. Strum told him it sounded like a good idea but that it was not feasible for the 1967 models at this time.

After the phone call, Strum met with Jack L. Smith and Gordon Cherry, two other product planning managers. They agreed that Yates' proposed car might have some market potential. But they also agreed that a car built exactly as Yates described would have too small a target market.

A brand-new kind of excitement.

and a great place to enjoy it.

Even great to be near.

Watch out. You're getting Dodge fever

Drive safely. It's also contagious

Dodge CHRYSLER MOTORS CORPORATION

'68 Dodge Coronet...your kind of beauty at your kind of price.

And you said, "It can't happen to me." Don't feel alone. You're with friends. Lots of them. That's how it is when you find a car like Dodge Coronet 500. It's more than just a new car . . . it's a new car with more.

Like more good looks. More extras. More safety items. More than you can resist. Strong V8 power. Deep-pile carpeting. Padded in-strument panel. In front—foam-padded, vinyl-trimmed bucket seats. Standard. (Optional on convertible and wagon models.) Or pick the optional fold-down center armrest-seat that makes room for three. (Three isn't a crowd in this one.)

Want to know more? Coronet comes in a full line of body styles—wagons, hardtops, con-vertibles, sedan, and new coupe. With a choice of 16 colors. And the power range goes from a 225-cubic-inch Six to a 440-cubic-inch Magnum V8. All at a price that won't strain your budget a bit. Now aren't you glad you've got Dodge Fever? Coronet makes it easy to cure. Just go see your nearby Dodge Dealer. Today.

Cherry was always a strong believer in gimmicks when it came to muscle cars. Young buyers, he believed, wanted all the hood scoops, decals, and big powerful engines their budgets would allow. For this car to succeed, Cherry believed it would need a full comple-ment of performance-look accessories. Foremost, however, the product would have to have a low production cost so that list price could also be low. Other-wise, the new model would be nothing

Non-muscle cars like this Coronet 500 were also included in 1968's "Dodge Fever" ad campaign. Chrysler

new in marketing. If the price exceeded a young buyer's means, Plymouth would miss the target market.

Smith drew up an add and delete sheet and concluded that the cheapest body style to produce was a two-door pillar coupe. Consequently, production

planners based the as-yet-unnamed Road Runner on the Belvedere pillar coupe. The Belvedere came standard with front bench seat done in cheap vinyl upholstery. By keeping this inte-

rior standard, great cost reductions could be had. Most of the production cost could be directed towards the engine, drivetrain, suspension, and brakes—a muscle car's heart.

It was agreed that the car's hood should have a "performance edge to it." But tooling up for an all-new hood would prove expensive beyond the model's budgeted cost. Since the 1968 models were being redesigned and the GTX was getting an all-new hood (with simulated hood vents that faced the side and carried the engine call-outs), the project would borrow the GTX's hood. Slight modifications to the Belvedere's

hood latch allowed the new GTX hood to fit.

The initial plan was to use the 440ci 375hp powerplant as the standard power unit. But this presented problems. The larger engine would be more expensive and marketing feared that it would cut too much into the GTX's sales. Smith proposed using the next biggest engine, a 383ci four-barrel V-8, but this was already an available engine option in the Belvedere line. And as Smith pointed out "the engine would have to be unique. Something that could not also be found in dad's sedan." Smith figured that swapping the 440's larger valve heads and camshaft would up the power output.

Engineering and Development bolted the 440 components to the 383 Super Commando V-8, but the dynamo test revealed that this alteration only increased horsepower by five. Although the Engineering department saw this as "an inconsequential increase," Smith assured them that it would be enough to give the buyer a feeling of more horsepower. Smith pointed out that the modified 383 could be used only in this model—it needed to be a feature unique to this car.

For years, all manufacturers, including Chrysler, had toyed with the name Road Runner as a model, but no one had seen the need to register it. In fact, the name appeared in a 1967 magazine ad for the Coronet R/T, which was ironic because it was about this time that Dodge found out that Plymouth was building the Road Runner. Was it a sales gimmick for the upcoming Road Runner, or was Dodge trying to upstage Plymouth before its release?

Many names had been drawn up and tested for the new Plymouth model including La Mancha, a name which Smith thought was absurd. Then one Saturday morning, Cherry was at home watching cartoons with his children. When a Road Runner cartoon came on, he watched the colorful bird screech to a stop and then take off down the road with lightning speed. Road Runner, he thought. That would be the perfect name for the new model. The following Monday he pitched his idea to Smith, who agreed.

Smith took advantage of the fact that no company had ever taken the Road Runner name seriously enough to register it with the Motor Vehicle Manufacturing Association. While he had a great model name, he knew that without the cartoon's likeness it would not have the same appeal. Plymouth had to have the rights to use the cartoon bird and coyote in ad campaigns. This way, every cartoon would be an advertisement for the car. Smith flew west to meet with Warner Brothers' attorneys, who at first were a little reluctant but ultimately signed a deal.

Next was a trip to Spartan, an electrical component manufacturer, to duplicate the bird's distinct sound for the car's horn. Two of the cartoon Road

Little production lead-time forced Plymouth stylists to use a black-and-white bird decal.

Runner's idiosyncrasies were his speed and that "beep beep." With a horn that imitated that sound, the image of the ultra-quick bird could be more easily tied to the Road Runner model. Chrysler spent over $50,000 reworking an old military horn to capture that peculiar sound. The horn was completed just short of the time when production was to begin, and Road Runner production began without ever testing the horn. Since a horn accounts for a part of the federally mandated safety equipment, all those involved took quite a gamble had the horn failed. The short development period explains why the horn was black in 1968 but purple with a "voice of the road Runner decal" from 1969 to 1974.

1968 Road Runner

The Road Runner used the low-trimmed Belvedere grille design (a large egg crate design with six vertical bars divided across the center by a single horizontal bar). Unlike the Belvedere, however, the Road Runner's grille was accented in black.

The hood featured two simulated hood scoops that sported the engine call-outs. If the "performance hood option" was selected the vents and the hood area between them was painted. This option was also available on the

GTX model. A decal of the cartoon Road Runner walking in place was put on each of the doors; standing bird decals were put on the deck lid and instrument panel. These decals were done in black and white, simply because time was running out and full-color decals with the bird in action would have to wait until the next model year. However, when a decor group was added to the coupe in early November 1967, a colorful bird depicted at full speed with a dust trail behind him was used on the deck lid trim. Road Runner nameplates were also placed on the doors and the deck lid just under the cartoon's likeness.

Inside, the scanty interior was done in either blue, parchment, or black and silver, which used an insert of black vinyl surrounded by a silver vinyl outer border. The instrument panel was the same as the one used in the Coronet R/T, but a 120mph speedometer was used instead of the R/T's 150mph unit. Because Plymouth did not yet have a version of the Charger's Rallye instrumentation, that instrument package was not available in the Road Runner. The steering wheel was a three-spoke

Inside, the 1968 Road Runner looked like a taxi cab. Only bench seating was available.

plastic rim wheel with no horn trim ring.

The Decor Group increased the color offerings to include gold, blue, red, green, all black, and white. The seats were done in a richer Ascot grain vinyl but they too were available only in bench seat form. Also included with this package was a color-keyed steering wheel with a partial horn ring, which was also available as a separate option, or a full horn ring steering wheel with a simulated wood rim wheel.

By mid-December 1967, a two-door hardtop was released. This model was based on the higher trimmed Satellite line and included the expanded color choice vinyl interior as standard equipment. However, bucket seats were not available as an option in this body style, either. No convertible Road Runners were built in 1968.

Power came from the special 383, which produced 335hp at 5200rpm and 425lbs-ft of torque at 3400rpm. The air cleaner used an ID tin that read "383 Road Runner engine" and also featured a black-and-white standing Road Runner cartoon likeness. The standard gearbox was a four-speed manual unit with an Inland brand shifter. Due to problems with these shifters, however, a Hurst shifter took its place shortly after the beginning of production. A column-mounted automatic was optional for both body styles, but no floor-shifted automatics were built.

Standard tires were F70x14in redlines, white-banded tires in the same size were a no-cost option. Tires were mounted on 14x5-1/2in wide steel wheels with dog dish hubcaps as standard fare. Full wheel covers and a set of dealer installed mag style wheel covers

Next page
Only a small "Hemi" badge on the deck lid told those being left behind what had just blown them off.

were optional. Only the awesome 426 Hemi was available as an option. Air conditioning was also optional, though only with the standard 383ci V-8 powerplant (it was not available with the Hemi). Other options included the same as those used on the Coronet models above.

1968 GTX: The Boss Is Back

Plymouth was still using the nickname "The Boss" in 1968, the year the GTX wore all new styling. The old unattractive boxy shape was gone. The lines were cleaner and rounder, which underscored the new look of the wider, lower design. Although the GTX and Coronet looked like siblings, the Ply-

The 1968 Plymouth's motivation source was proudly called out on the sides of the hood vents. This model could frighten any wily coyote.

mouths used more of the popular Coke bottle styling in the rear roof area. Speed lines were placed high on the front fenders and rear quarter panels, which gave the impression of movement even when standing still. These design features were also carried over to the Road Runner.

The GTX's grille consisted of thin horizontal blades with the GTX name placed in the center. As with all B-bodies, small round side lamps were placed on the front fenders and the rear quarter panels. Twin racing stripes were placed along the lower side of the

body beginning just behind the front wheelwell and ending just in front of the rear quarter panels' GTX emblems. These stripes came in red, white, blue, or black. The GTX nameplate was also carried on a special trim panel on the rear deck lid. This panel was accented with red tape.

Inside, the GTX was understated in a way that would have been more at home in a luxury car than a muscle car. The carpeting was a cut deep pile, and the standard bucket seats were covered in rich, lightly sculpted vinyl. The instrument panel was trimmed with Mylar-covered simulated walnut grain, the door panels were accented with flat black trim. The instrumentation was the same as that on the Coronet R/T including the 150mph speedometer and optional tachometer or clock. Like the

Road Runner, the Rallye instrumentation package was not available with the GTX. Buyers had the choice of eight interior colors and eighteen exterior shades, including an extra-cost, hand-buffed silver metallic. The same exterior colors were available on all the B-bodys. Bench seating was not available as an option, but a center fold-down seat cushion/armrest was. A center console was also optional, but was not available if the center armrest was selected.

Hardtop models could be optioned with a black, white, or green vinyl roof. Convertibles came with a black or white, power-operated top. Mechanically, the GTX was basically unchanged, but the standard 440 Super Commando was restyled. The heads were no longer unique, and though the new heads

The 1968 GTX wore all new sleek styling and was the only Belvedere-based muscle car to come standard with the 440ci Super Commando V-8. Chrysler

flowed less freely than 1967's, the horsepower rating remained the same (the 1967 440 had been conservatively rated). A column-shifted automatic remained standard, and the four-speed manual was a no-cost option. As in 1967, the Hemi suspension was standard with F70x14in redline tires. When the Hemi was installed in any B-body, including the Dodges, F70x15in tires mounted on 15x6in steel wheels came standard . Power front disc brakes were optional on all models as was tinted glass. The power disc brakes were standard on the Hemi-equipped Charger.

1969 Charger: Refining the Great One

The 1968 Charger was such a sales success—with an astounding increase of 343 percent over 1967—that it was voted "Success Car of the Year" by Dodge's fellow automobile manufacturers. Changes that occurred to the 1969

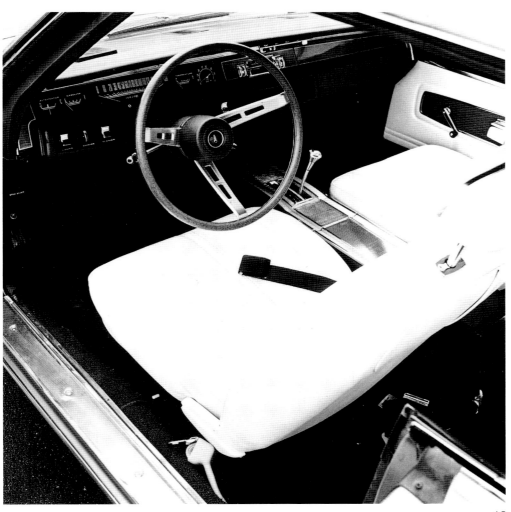

The GTX interior was just the opposite of the Road Runner. Rich, luxurious buckets were the only seating available. Chrysler

The chrome road wheel was a popular option.

Charger were characterized by Bill Brownlie as "natural evolution in design."

The hideaway headlamps remained, but the grille was split by a center divider bar that featured gills cut into the sides. The bar gave the Charger a twin venturi look. (Plymouth would borrow this concept for the 1973 Plymouth Barracuda grille.) The dull silver bar contrasted handsomely with the dark-colored grille background. The same emblems were used on the grille as in 1968, but they were repositioned to the driver's side headlamp door.

As with all B-bodys, the round side lamps were replaced with rectangular

The 1969 Charger's appearance went through "natural evolution" which included a center divider for the grille and rectangular side-marker lights. Chrysler

shape units situated lower on the body. The round taillamps were replaced with two long thin rectangular shaped ones that narrowed slightly towards the inward side. In between the taillamps was the Charger script and medallion on all models except the Charger R/T, which used a single R/T emblem. There were no other significant exterior changes.

The interior was mostly unchanged from 1968. Two exceptions were the use of a new upholstery design that used pleating of small squares and the deletion of the clock as standard equipment. Even the door panels were an exact copy in design from those used the previous year.

To give the Charger a more "personal car feel," the Special Edition (SE) package was created. This option was crafted mainly by the Interior Design Studio and included leather and vinyl front bucket seats in either black, tan, blue, or red; the rear bench seat remained all vinyl. This package also included simulated woodgrain on the instrument panel; a walnut rim steering wheel; bright trim around the pedals; full-wheel, deep dish wheel covers; hood-mounted turn indicators; and "Special Edition" badges placed on the C-pillars, replacing the Charger script. The SE package was available on any Charger model, this would be the only year it was available on the base Charger. Also available with all models except those with the SE package was a cloth and vinyl interior done in black only.

Mechanically, the Charger was unchanged except that the standard powerplant for the base Charger was now a 225ci slant six-cylinder rated at 145hp at 4000rpm. But Charger owners were not interested in economy, and fewer than 500 Chargers were equipped with the standard slant six.

Charger 500 and Daytona: Race Cars for the Street

While the Charger's appearance was at the forefront of design, it was a hindrance on NASCAR's banked ovals. The 1968 Charger won only two races and neither of them was at a major track.

Chrysler's Racing Engineer Bob Rodger was determined to put Dodge back into the winner's circle. He or-

dered wind tunnel testing, which showed that the deeply inset grille and tunnel backlight hampered the car's ability to slice through the wind. The front end acted like a scoop, catching air instead of allowing it to flow smoothly over the hood. The critically acclaimed rear glass created a low pressure that induced excessive drag.

This 1969 ad emphasized the 1969 Charger R/T's handling. Chrysler

Rodger figured that if the grille and the rear glass were made flush with the body contours, the 1969 design could gain 5mph over the 1968's top end. Rodger used a 1968 Coronet grille and special mounting brackets that brought it out flush with the hood. He molded in a cap on the roof into which was installed a flush-mounted back glass. Because the new rear glass extended further into the rear deck area, a new trunk lid had to be used. Wide moldings over the front windshield pillars helped smooth air flow over the roof. These measures greatly improved the Charger's aerodynamics.

NASCAR homologation rules required that a certain number of cars on which racers would be based had to be sold to the public before competition by that model would be permitted. Although this did not mean that all production models had to be offered to the public, it certainly meant that the greatest portion should be. According to Chrysler, 392 Charger 500s were built

This is the first Charger 500 built, now owned by Mike Russo. Note the wheel covers that replaced the original, recalled cast-aluminum wheels. This photo was taken when the car still belonged to Dodge. Chrysler

The First Charger 500

There was nothing odd about the Dodge News Bureau in New York City ordering a car to be used for magazine road tests. Hence, no eyebrows were raised when the bureau ordered two 1969 Charger 500s in the latter part of 1968. Both cars were painted Bright Red with bumble bee stripes and equipped, like all early 500s, with the 426 Hemi powerplant. One car was a basic model with an automatic transmission, the other had a four-speed manual.

For the four-speed car, however, the News Bureau marked off options, you would not expect to find on a Charger 500. Ultimately, the order blank looked like this:

1969 Charger 500	$3,843.00
AO1 Light Package	25.95
A34 Super Track Pack	256.45
B41 Front Disc Brakes	50.15
B51 Power Brakes	42.95
C16 Console	54.45
C31 Head Rests	26.50
C5X Cloth/Vinyl Interior	no cost
D21 Four Speed	no cost
E74 426 Hemi	648.20
G11 Tinted Glass	40.70
G33 Remote LH Mirror	10.45
J55 Hood Pad/Under Coating	16.60
L31 Hood Turn Indicators	10.80
N85 Tachometer/clock	50.15
P31 Power Windows	105.20
R21 AM/FM Radio	134.95
S77 Power Steering	99.99
S81 Wood Rim Steering Wheel	26.75
W23	127.95
TOTAL	$5,571.19

After receiving finishing touches at the Hamtrack, Michigan, assembly plant, it made its debut to a group of magazine writers. But before the car could be tested, the cast aluminum wheels were replaced by stamped steel wheels with deluxe wheel covers (reports said that the aluminum wheels could fail). Several magazines tested the car, including Car Life and Hot Rod, before it was offered for sale as a used car.

On June 28, 1970, Mike Russo was out driving with a friend when they blew by Turnpike Auto Sales. From the corner of his eye, Russo spotted a flash of red car as they passed the lot. He whipped his car around, turned into the driveway, and ran over to the car. "Hemi"—a word that even then would cause your heartbeat to quicken—was written across the windshield in white lettering. He cupped his hands over his eyes and peered through the tinted glass at the odometer: only 13,000 miles!

He asked the lot owner the price and he was told $5,000. Russo began to haggle and eventually he and the owner settled at $3,145. Since Russo couldn't get to his bank until the next day, he borrowed ten dollars from his friend, gave it to the owner, and had him hold the car. The next day he arrived, cash in hand, and took ownership of the 1969 Charger Hemi 500.

The following Saturday was the fourth of July. Mike found himself and his car as much a part of the festivities as the fireworks lighting up the New York City sky. Other Hemi owners checked out Russo's car and were amused with his amazement at the Hemi. However, neither Russo nor his fellow Hemi fans knew the car's story at that time. If they had, Russo's friends would have been the ones in amazement, for the car that Russo owned and still owns was not only the Charger they had all read about in the magazines, but it was also the first Charger 500 built.

Today, Russo has seen fit to share his treasure with the rest of the world. With the help of Hurst, Kelsey Tire Co., Year One, Charger Specialties, Master Power Brake Co., and Legendary Interiors, he restored the first Charger 500 and donated it to the Weedsport Auto Museum in Weedsport, New York.

Unique badges on the C-pillars identified the Special Edition Charger package.

Mother warned me...

that there would be men like you driving cars like that. Do you really think you can get to me with that long, low, tough machine you just rolled up in? Ha! If you think a girl with real values is impressed by your air conditioning and stereo . . . a 440 Magnum, whatever that is . . . well, it takes more than cushy bucket seats to make me flip. Charger R/T SE. Sounds like alphabet soup. Frankly, I'm attracted to you because you have a very intelligent face. My name's Julia.

Join the fun . . . catch

Not an ad that would play in 1993, but undoubtedly very hip in 1969. Chrysler

for US shipment. Some were shipped to Canada while others were intended for racing. In total, roughly 450 Charger 500s were sold; fewer than the 500 minimum required for racing homologation. It is believed that the remaining fifty Charger 500s were converted to Daytonas when the switch in racing was made.

Chrysler farmed out the cars to Creative Industries in Detroit for modification. Initially, the 426 Hemi was the standard powerplant with no optional engine. When these were first being sold, they had a low profile and were intended for racing purposes only. But when it seemed that too few would be sold, the 440 Magnum was made the standard engine with the Hemi as the only optional powerplant. This increased sales because the price was less for the 440-equipped car. Standard wheels were 15x6in stamped steel units initially, but when the 440 Magnum became standard this was changed to 14in wheels. For identification, a 500 nameplate was placed on the grille and the rear deck lid. Also, wider body sill moldings and wide A-pillar molding were used to improve airflow over the car.

Rear bumble bee identification stripes were added to models destined for the public.

Dodge Charger: The Movie Star

The Dodge Charger was such a success that it became the star of two movies. The first was Director Peter Yate's 1968 release Bullitt.. The movie starred Steve McQueen, who played a San Francisco cop named Lieutenant Frank Bullitt, on the trail of hired killers. Ask anyone what they remember about this movie and nine times out of ten the answer will be "the car chase." Hailed at the time as the all-time best car chase ever filmed, it put the viewer right into the car.

The car that chased Bullitt (who in turn begins to chase it) is a Jewel Black 1968 Charger R/T with a black vinyl top and black interior and without the rear bumble bee stripes. It was powered by a 440 Magnum V-8 with a four-speed transmission. Other options on the car were deep dish style wheel covers, which it lost during the chase, and

hood-mounted turn indications. The chase ends with the Charger plowing into a gas pump and exploding into a fireball. Many believe that a Hemi powered this car, but that is not the case.

The next time a Dodge Charger appeared in a film was in 1974's Dirty Mary and Crazy Larry, starring Peter Fonda as a would-be stock car driver. Adam Roarke costarred as his mechanic, and Susan George costarred as a one-night stand who decides to stay around.

Fonda and Roarke rob a supermarket by holding the store manger's wife hostage. With the law in hot pursuit, the two dump their 1967 Impala Super Sport for a 1969 Charger R/T. The Dodge is painted light green with a custom hockey stick stripe and the 440 lettering done in black along the sides of the car (a couple of yellow cars were also used in the movie). The wheels were American brand slotted mags. Inside was a black interior, shoulder

straps, and an automatic transmission with a a floor-mounted shifter.

One by one, they outrun the police while trying to reach a section of land where there are an endless number of roads. One officer, knowing that he has lost them, tricks them into running into a freight train. Once again, the Charger explodes into a fireball.

The 1969 Dodge Charger became a star of the small screen when CBS added "The Dukes of Hazzard " to its Friday night lineup. Without a doubt, the show's centerpiece was the Hemi Orange 1969 Charger—called the General Lee—with a confederate flag painted on the roof and the number "01" on the sides. The series was famous for its outrageous car leaps, which, unfortunately, destroyed each car upon landing. The show destroyed so many 1969 Chargers that towards the end the prop department used AMC Ambassadors painted to match the original General Lee.

The Charger 500 made its racing debut on February 1, 1969, at the "Motor Trend 500" in Riverside, California. Buddy Baker captured the pole position, Bobby Isaac sat in the number two spot, and Charlie Glotzbach was in the fourth position—all drivers were in Charger 500s. It looked like Dodge might capture first, second, and third place. When the checkered flag was just about to drop, however, Cale Yarborough's Ford Torino blew by Glotzbach terminating Dodge's trip to the winner's circle.

The next week, Bobby Allison was edged out of a win by David Pearson's Ford. Rodger was truly disappointed that the Charger 500 was not performing as well as he had hoped. The 5mph increase was there, but the sleek, fastback Fords were overwhelming it.

Daytona: With a Wing and Prayer

Because the Charger 500 was not quite the race success for which Dodge had hoped, a new plan was devised. After additional wind tunnel testing, it was decided to graft an aerodynamic nose onto the front of the Charger to further improve air flow and increase top speed. A nose was quickly built and wind tunnel testing began again.

Tests showed that while air flowed smoothly over the nose, it was being disturbed at the car's tail, creating a deadly oversteer problem. Bob Rodger looked at the Chaparral race car with its high wing spoiler and figured this could be adapted to the Charger's body. Placing the wing high enough above the car, where the wind was clean, would apply a down force to the car overcoming the unbalanced condition. Rearward facing scoops were also placed on the front fenders to allow engine heat to escape (the scoops on public versions, however, were not functional).

Final testing was done at the Chelsea, Michigan, test track where Charlie Glotzbach reached a speed of 193mph before the Hemi blew apart. The name *Daytona* was just a continuation of the "500" name—as in Daytona 500. It was also a response to the Ford Torinos, which were called Talladegas. Ironically, Talladega, NASCAR'S newest track, would be the site of Dodge's first strike at Ford.

Rodger discovered that air flowed smoothly over the Charger if it had a flush backlight.

Next page
A shark-like nose allowed the Daytona to slice cleanly through the wind.

The wide, wing-colored stripe carried the model's name.

On September 9, 1969, seven winged warriors were trailered into the garage area of the Alabama International Speedway in Talladega, including two owned by Dodge Motors. That year, however, various drivers boy-

Rear-facing, fender-mounted scoops acted as exhaust vents for engine heat in the race cars, but were non-functional on the street version.

Next page
The towering rear wing made the Daytona unbeatable. The wing's angle could be adjusted by loosening the screws that attached the wing's horizontal piece to the vertical stabilizers.

The Daytona's interior was the same as any other Charger.

cotted the race track because they felt it was too rough and unsafe at high speeds. As a result, only the two Dodge-owned cars remained on that following Sunday: purple number 99 driven by Glotzbach and red-and-white number 71 driven by Bobby Isaac.

Glotzbach joined the boycott the Saturday night before the race, and Dodge asked Richard Brickhouse to drive number 99. He agreed. At the time,

This winged warrior was driven to victory at the first Talladega 500 by Richard Brickhouse after the car's intended driver, Charlie Glotzbach, joined other drivers in a boycott of the race. Chrysler

Bobby Allison was another driver who saw the advantage of Dodge's design. Chrysler

he said, "With the chance to drive a factory car, I think anybody in the same position would have done the same thing." Brickhouse went on to win the race; Isaac came in fourth. The two 1969 Charger 500s came in second and third. Dodge had swept the race just as Rodger had wanted.

The Daytona demonstrated that it was the king of the high banks at the end of the season at College Station, Texas. Bobby Isaac lapped Donnie Allison's Ford twice before taking the checkered flag.

1969 Coronet R/T and Super Bee

A new grille and taillamps adorned the mid-sized Dodges for 1969. The grille used a deep inset delta shape with horizontal blades that bent outwards in the center and along the axis. The R/T wore a red-and-black "R/T" nameplate on the grille's left-hand side, while the Super Bee had a Bumble Bee-shaped emblem in the same location. This Bee emblem had been planned for the 1968 model but, like the Road Runner emblem, time ran out and it had to be held over for the next year.

The standard hood was unchanged from 1968 with the center dome and simulated vents. But a new option called Ram Charger allowed the engine

to receive fresh air. This required a special hood with cutouts covered by wedge-shaped hood scoops. The scoops forced air into the carburetor via plastic duct work bolted to the hood's underside. A special open-element air cleaner connected to this duct with a rubber seal that directed the incoming air down the carburetor's throat. Special "doors" just below the hood scoops and a switch on the instrument panel allowed the driver to control whether the engine received cool, fresh air or air heated by the engine. "This package," Brownlie recalled, "was for high visibility and drawn up by the people in the Marketing and Engineering departments." To further improve the visibility factor, engine call-outs were placed on the outward side of each scoop.

Except for the change to rectangular side lamps, the body sides remained unaltered from 1968. Each model used a diametrically opposite tail end design. The Super Bee used a system of two concave taillamps covered with trim, which divided the rear light unit so that each assembly looked like three separate lenses. The Dodge name was spelled out between the taillamps. On the deck lid's right-hand edge was a small bumble bee emblem.

The Coronet R/T models used a different set of taillamps to differentiate it from the low-trimmed Coronets. The taillamps were long, thin, rectangular units with no bezel. Between the taillamps was a red reflective lens that matched the taillamps' design and shape. When headlamps from another car hit the rear light assembly, the R/T gave the impression of three taillamps.

Because of the center reflector, the Dodge name was moved up to the center of the deck lid edge, followed by an R/T emblem. The bumble bee stripes were again standard in either black, white, or red. The stripes were now solid with the R/T cutout on the quarter stripes. The Super Bee used similar stripes, with the Super Bee logo on the sides. The stripes could be deleted, but with the Super Bee the round decal logo was still used. If stripes were deleted on a Coronet R/T, an emblem was placed on the rear quarter panels just behind the rear wheelwell openings.

A dress-up option on both Coronet models was scoops placed over the simulated vents on the rear quarter panels. These were part of a Dodge deluxe package.

The Coronet R/T was offered in the same body styles as 1968, but a hardtop coupe was added to the Super Bee lineup in addition to the pillar coupe. Even though Plymouth offered a convertible version of the Road Runner in 1969, a drop top for the Super Bee was never considered. Said Brownlie, "The convertible was on its way out. They were leaky and drafty. And government regulations were killing the convertible."

The topless Charger show car in 1969 was just that according to Brownlie. "It was built only for the Auto

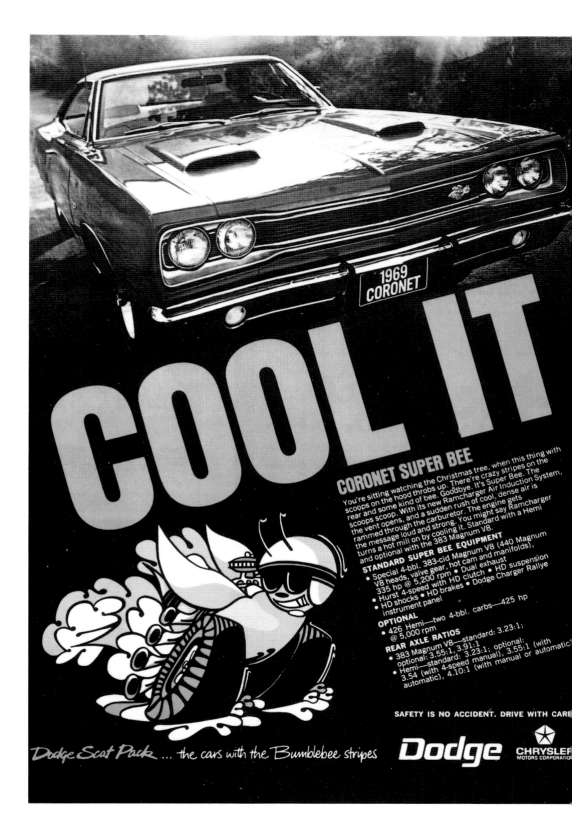

This ad appeared in the October 1968 issue of Car and Driver and announced the availability of the Ram Charger hood scoop package. Chrysler

Functional hood scoops on the Coronet models were new options for 1969. They also held the engine call outs.

Show," he said. "It was in no way intended that the Charger might be offered as a convertible. We ourselves [the car manufacturers] killed the convertible with the introduction of the two-door hardtop, as it allowed air to flow through without the problems of the convertible."

1969 Plymouth: And the Beat Goes On

By 1969 Plymouth was using the cartoon Road Runner and Wile E. Coyote likenesses to sell not only the Road Runner but all Plymouths. A television

Next page
A special air cleaner was required for R/Ts equipped with the functional hood scoops.

A true bumble bee emblem was used on the 1969 Super Bees.

Twin simulated air vents on the rear quarter panels were optional on both Coronet models.

The Coronet R/T used a center reflector to give the appearance of three taillamps.

Previous page
The Coronet R/T was the only Dodge mid-sized muscle car available as a convertible.

The Coronet R/T's interior was trimmed with simulated walnut to give it an upscale look.

ad showed the bird running into a Plymouth dealership looking over the newly styled Furys, Barracudas, and, of course, the mid-sized Belvederes. The coyote, meanwhile, was in pursuit, running into the Furys' doors and finally ending up locked in the trunk of a red Belvedere by the quick-witted bird. The

A hardtop model joined the pillar coupe in the 1969 Super Bee lineup. No convertible Bees were ever built. Chrysler

Functional hood scoops were available on the Plymouth models, too, where it was known as the Air Grabber.

Using this instrument panel-mounted control, the driver could turn the fresh-air flow to the carburetors on or off.

ads were all created to promote the great Plymouth Sale.

1969 GTX: Subtle Changes

Continuing into its third year, the GTX used the same styling it had in 1968. The grille was restyled using two red-accented horizontal bars which contoured outward at the grille's center and supported the GTX nameplate. The lower body sill moldings and twin body side stripes were eliminated and replaced with reflective body side stripes in either red or white outlined by bright moldings on the lower portion of the body.

The GTX nameplate was still used on the rear quarter panels. The car's tail was cleaned up with a single red accented trim panel embossed with the

GTX name in the center. Backup lamps were moved to the rear bumper. The Plymouth name was placed on the deck lid's right side.

Unlike the Coronet, the GTX hood was completely restyled. It featured two simulated vents whose openings faced upward instead of to the sides. Engine call-out badges were still placed along the vents' sides. Two types of trim were used on top of the hood vents. A black accent cover was standard with the 440ci V-8. The Coronet's fresh air hood scoop option was called the Air Grabber when installed in a Plymouth. When this option was selected, screens replaced the standard vents' covers, thus making the vents functional. The Air Grabber was standard with the 426 Hemi. Like the Coronet, this option used a system of underhood duct

Previous page
A new grille highlighted the GTX in its third year of production.

Beware Killer Bees and Vicious Birds

In 1967 General Motors announced that multi-carburetors would be eliminated from all cars except the Corvette. At the same time, Ford was phasing out their twin four-barrel 427ci V-8 from production. This left Chrysler—and its 426 Hemi—with just about the only multi-carburetor-equipped engine on the market. Knowing that nothing says "hot rod" like multi-carbs, they continued the option. But the Hemi was really only for those wanting an all-out street racer—it was out of most buyers' price range. Hoping to entice some consumers who wanted multi-carbs but could not afford a Hemi, Engineering and Product Planning managers worked together to create an affordable engine with multi-carburetion.

The engineers began with the 440 high-performance V-8. To this they added a few touches, including an Edelbrock high-rise aluminum manifold and three two-barrel Holley carburetors. Then they looked into their own high-performance parts bin and added Hemi head valve springs and retainers. They also added valves with flash-chromed stems, molybdenum-filled piston rings, a more radical cam, and a dual-point distributor. All these modifications added up to 390hp at 4700rpm and 390lbs-ft of torque at 3600rpm. This was an ideal power range; everyday drivers noticed the increased power more than they would with the higher-revving Hemi. Chrysler even billed it as the "poor man's Hemi."

The Product Planning department now stepped in. Dodge chose the Super Bee to receive the modified engine because it was the most popular with the street racing crowd and would permit the lowest introductory cost. To give the Super Bee that drag strip look, a fiberglass hood with a large, center-mounted, functional air scoop was designed. Fiberglass was chosen because it was more economical to mold a new hood than to cast a new steel one. Fiberglass body panels were also a popular weight-saving trick employed by racers. But weight reduction was not Dodge's goal—looks and low cost were. The look and low cost was also the reason Dodge held the hood in place with four NASCAR style hood pins. They added a racy look, plus saved the additional cost that reinforc-

continued on next page

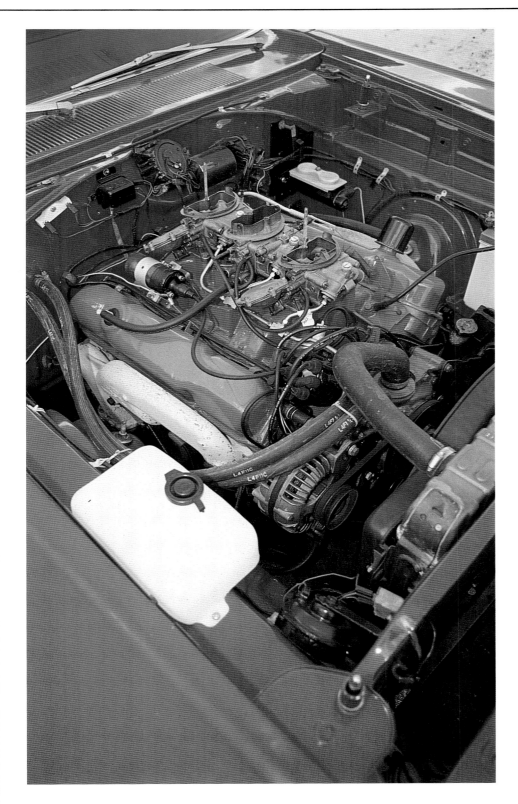

Rated at 390hp, this engine was fed by three two-barrel Holley carburetors.

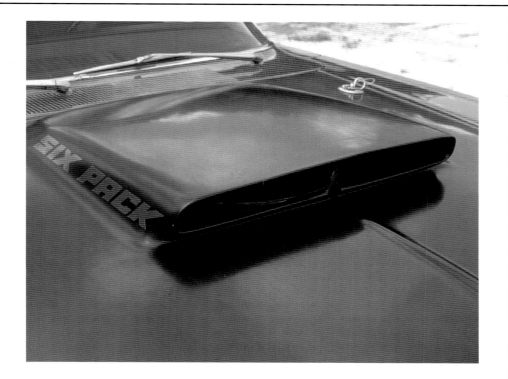

A Fiberglass hood added to the car's drag racer look.

ing the hood would have required had hinges been used.

A trip to the drag strip showed that racers were running slicks mounted to stamped steel wheels. To duplicate this look with street tires, product planning swapped in 15in stamped steel wheels from the Hemi-equipped cars and added chrome lug nuts to lend a more aggressive appearance.

The interior was limited to either black or white in standard bench or front bucket seats. The exterior was painted Bright Red, Bright Green, Bright Yellow, or Hemi Orange. Bumble Bee stripes were available in either black or white. No 440 six-pack Super Bees were built with the red bumble bee stripes. A vinyl top was available but only in black or white.

Certain options were not available. These included air conditioning, disc brakes, road wheel or wheel covers, other tires (G70x15in blackwalls were

standard), any other axle packages (Dana 9 3/4in with 4.10 gears were standard with either the four speed or automatic), fresh-air hood, automatic speed control, or trailering package.

Dodge offered the multi-carb 440 package on either the two-door hardtop or the pillar coupe Super Bee models. Plymouth also got into the act and offered nearly the same package on the Road Runner using the same body styles. No 440 six-pack convertibles were built. The same color trim and exterior colors used on the Dodge were offered on the Road Runners. The biggest difference is the hood. The Dodges used a red decal that read "Six Pack" while the Plymouths read "440 6bl." Of the two models, the Dodge received the most press and sold the most units. In fact, Dodge sold more hardtops alone than Plymouth did in both body styles combined.

The A12 Super Bee with the 440 six-pack V-8 was marketed as a Chrysler package car. A Road Runner with the same engine was also available.

work to direct air into the carburetor. As with Dodge's version, the driver could open or close the vents with a switch on the instrument panel.

1969 Road Runner: Add a Drop Top

In 1969, the Road Runner only got better. In addition to coupe and hardtop versions, a convertible was added to the Road Runner's lineup. Mechanically, the Road Runner, or the "Beep Beep" as it was called by the street set, was unchanged from 1968 with the 383ci 335hp V-8 standard on all body styles. The standard GTX-style hood was fitted to all 383-equipped versions, but 383 engine call-outs appeared on the vents' sides instead of the 440 emblems carried on the GTX. Like the GTXs, 426 Hemi-powered Road Runners came standard with the Air Grabber hood; here the name "Hemi" was placed on the sides of the scoops.

In addition to the hood, another exterior change was a restyled grille. The insert featured a single horizontal bar divided in half by a single vertical bar. No nameplate appeared on the grille.

At the rear, the taillamps were restyled and inset deeper than previously. The deck lid was clean except for the Road Runner name on the far right-hand side. A full-color decal of the cartoon character holding a racing helmet was placed in the center of the deck lid; this same decal was also used on the instrument panel. The nameplate and decals on the doors were also restyled. The bird was now in color, running at full speed with a dust trail in his wake. Placed just behind the bird was the Road Runner nameplate. These were two separate, freestanding emblems which were stamped into a rectangular backing plate.

Motor Trend magazine found this car so outstanding that they awarded it "Car of the Year" honors for 1969. Ellen Merlo, managing editor of *Motor Trend* at the time, said the Road Runner was "definitely the best car to come out of Detroit this year."

This is one of only thirteen Charger R/Ts built with a Hemi powerplant and the Special Edition package.

Unfortunately, Plymouth's public success was not mirrored at the race track. While Dodge was tearing up the NASCAR season with their Daytona, Plymouth could not manage even one win. A good reason for the losing record was the absence of driver Richard Petty, who had switched to Ford for his oval exploits.

1970: The Last of the Classic Style

By the end of the decade, muscle cars were showing up on everyone's hit list. Safety zealots in the government called muscle cars unsafe, gross polluters. Insurance companies regarded them as high risks.

All B-bodies received minor changes for 1970. The body side lamps were made bigger and positioned farther down on the body. Mechanically, the 440 six-pack V-8 was now a regular production option and was available across the board for all models except the base Charger and new Charger 500 models. The new 500 was related to its ancestor only in name, as it used the production Charger's grille and tunneled in backlight.

1970 Charger: The Grand Champion

The Charger was given a mild face lift for 1970, with a full width single-opening grille trimmed in silver across the horizontal center. The Charger script was placed on the main grille section once again and the sub-model designation on the left headlamp door. A total of three sub-models were available: the base Charger, the Charger R/T, and the Charger 500. The entire grille was encircled by a single-loop front bumper. Because of its late introduction into the 1970 NASCAR season, many feel the Daytona was a 1970 model. Although sales material listed it as such, no 1970 Daytonas were built. In fact, all Daytonas were built in 1969 before the car debuted at the Talladega racetrack.

Scallops were continued on the doors of all Chargers. However, those on the Charger R/T were covered by fiberglass rear facing scoops that also wore a large R/T emblem. Because of

All higher trimmed Charger models used special trim around the taillamps.

Bucket seats were still standard with the Charger R/T models. This one uses leather trim, which was part of the SE package.

the scoop's location, those Charger R/Ts that were equipped with a Hemi engine could no longer use a Hemi badge on the doors as they had in previous years; so the badge was made larger and placed on the forward edge of the front fenders. Charger script was still used on the C-pillar of all models and was also used between the taillamps, not unlike 1968, with the sub-model emblem following it. The taillamps looked like those used in 1969 but are actually

different. Those models without the Special Dodge trim package were accented with argent silver paint and used bright trim around the taillamps. This trim was standard on the Charger R/Ts and optional on the Charger 500.

The rear bumble bee stripes were revised and were now a single solid stripe with no side ID cutouts flanked by two thinner stripes. Color choice was expanded to include blue and green in addition to the carryover white, red, and black. Also available at the R/T customer's request were longitude stripes. These stripes were available in the same colors as the bumble bee stripes, but they wrapped around the

Next page
Air cleaners were restyled in 1970.

side door scoops and traced the body contour lines back to the rear edge of the quarter panels.

Inside, the base Charger lost its standard front bucket seats. Now a split-back all-vinyl bench seat was standard. The Charger 500 and Charger R/T were again standard with front bucket seats. The door panels were slightly restyled: the upper section still used the Charger medallion, and a Charger script name was added to the lower portion of the door panel. The

78

black or tan; chrome trim around the pedals; simulated walnut rim steering wheel; simulated walnut trim on the instrument panel (this trim was standard on the Charger R/T models); the light group (which included a light under the top of the instrument panel); deep dish wheel covers; and vinyl map pockets on the doors (these had been standard on all Chargers in 1968 and 1969 but were now available only with the Charger SE package).

An option that became available on the late-built 1969 models was black tape stripes placed in the lower depressions of the Charger's hood. This continued into 1970 until it was replaced near the end of December with tape graphics. The new graphics called out the engine ID in broad, bold letters or numbers done in silver reflective tape. This was coded as the Charger's version of the "Performance Hood" option. It was available only on the Charger R/T model and the decal read either "440" with the standard engine or the 440 six-pack or "Hemi" when the 426 Hemi was placed under the scalloped hood.

1970 Coronet R/T and Super Bee: The Last in Line

Sales for the Coronet R/T were never truly strong. In 1968 it went into a slump due to the Charger and the Super Bee models taking away buyers—1970 would mark its last year as a model.

For its final stand, the Coronet R/T received a major facelift. A dominant design feature was a split front bumper and grille arrangement. The grille and the headlamp bezels were combined into one unit on each side of the car. The two grille and front bumper loops were divided by the beak that curved downward on the front of the hood, where it met a filler panel. The submodel nameplate was placed on this beak—an R/T emblem in the case of the Coronet R/T and a bumble bee on wheels emblem for the Super Bee. The R/T's hood featured a center domed section with simulated twin air scoops, which looked similar to air inlets under a fighter jet's wings.

The Coronet R/T had no emblems placed on the sides of the scoops while the Super Bee had its model name placed there. The Ram Charger hood

This Hemi hood graphic was a midyear option for the Charger R/T only.

Special Edition package option continued but was available only on the Charger R/T and Charger 500 models. It included front bucket seats with leather inserts in either green, blue, option continued and was identical in operation to that used in 1969—it even used the same hood scoops. When the Ram Charger option was selected, the engine call-out was placed on the outboard sides of each scoop. Coronets fitted with the 426 Hemi powerplant came standard with the Ram Charger hood and used the name "Hemi" instead of an engine call-out. The "440" call-outs were used with both the Coronet's standard 440 Magnum or the 440 six-pack. A 440 four-barrel V-8 was not available for the Super Bee, and the 440 call-outs were used only when the car was built with the 440 six-pack powerplant.

Rear-facing scoops similar to those on the Charger's doors were placed over the restyled simulated air vents on the Coronet R/T's rear quarter panels. A red-and-black R/T nameplate was worn by this scoop. These scoops were not available on the Super Bee models as standard equipment or as a dress-up package option as in the year before.

The Coronet R/T used the same bumble bee stripes as the Charger R/T and they were available in the same choice of colors. Longitude stripes were not available for the Coronet R/T model. The Super Bee used the same stripes it had in 1969, but, like the other Dodge models, expanded the color choice to include green and blue. All stripe colors used a round Super Bee logo; however, the logo was available in black or white only. No red, green, or blue Super Bee logos were made. When the red, blue, or green stripes were ordered, a white logo was used with dark color exteriors and a black logo with light colored exteriors.

Unlike its big brother, but like the Charger R/T, the Super Bee had alternative stripe patterns. The reverse C-Stripes, as they are commonly called, included two hockey stick stripes that trace the contours of the rear quarter panel. They begin at the front edge of the panel and widen as they move towards the car's rear where the lower stripe curves upward and the upper stripe curves downward. The place the two stripes meet is divided by the Super Bee logo. These stripes were available in the same colors as the bumble bee stripes and they too only used either a black or white Super Bee logo.

Inside, the 1970 Coronet was basically a copy of the 1968 model, including instrumentation. The Charger's Rallye gauges were standard in the Super Bee and optional in the Coronet R/T, which still used the same gauge package it did in 1968. The door panels were restyled; the Super Bee used a panel with thin vertical pleats and the Coronet R/T had wider vertical pleats. The Coronet R/T nameplate was placed on a trim piece above the glovebox door. The glovebox door was also restyled and now used a plastic shell hinged more conventionally at the bottom instead of the top as had been the practise in 1968 and 1969. Vinyl bench

Three views of the 1970 Coronet R/T. Note that simulated hood and side scoops were still part of the muscle car look. Chrysler

seating was still standard in the Super Bee with front bucket seats an option. Buckets were standard in the Coronet R/T. A console or a center folding armrest was optional for either model.

1970: Plymouth Makes It

In 1969, Plymouth's General Manager Glenn White called Richard Petty in an attempt to woo him back to the make that had put him in the winner's circle so many times (including the

The 1970 Super Bee was the only Coronet model available with an alternative striping pattern. Chrysler

The Super Bird racer was designed to lure Richard Petty back to Plymouth. To meet homologation requirements, nearly 2,000 Super Birds were offered to the public.

record-breaking 1967 season). White told Petty that Plymouth was working on a car to be campaigned during the 1970 race season that would be similar to the Dodge Daytona.

Petty had a one year, renewable contract with Ford, but he chose to jump ship when Plymouth offered a Daytona clone. Petty believed, as did many other racers, that the Daytona

held a special design advantage over other racers.

Dodge definitely had a head start over Plymouth at the racetrack because they had worked out all of the Daytona's bugs. Plymouth also labored under new homologation rules which required it to sell twice as many units as Dodge. The new rules were based on

Like the Daytona, the Super Bird used retractable headlamps.

Although it looks identical to the Daytona's wing, the Super Bird's has more rake.

the number of dealers selling the manufacturer's brand. This was extremely tough on Ford Motor Company and General Motors. Both Ford and Chevrolet would have had to sell over 5,000 units each. Consequently both companies abandoned any projects aimed at the Daytona. Ford continued with the Talladegas and Mercury Cyclones for one more year.

Plymouth decided to copy the Daytona and do it quickly so that it would qualify for the Motor Trend 500 at Riverside, California, on January 18, 1970. But since Plymouth had no Charger clone, the design had to be modified for its B-body hardtop coupe. Dodge used the Charger, its best-selling performance model, as the base, so Plymouth used the Road Runner, its best-selling model, as its base. Initially, Plymouth planned to use the GTX as the base because that was the car most frequently used by racers. However, sales of nearly 2,000 GTXs would have been required to meet the new homologation rules, and Plymouth officials

feared a GTX-based winged car might not sell.

The Road Runner was not a Charger clone, so Plymouth had to revamp the Daytona's design to fit the Road Runner's body. A nose was designed and built only to find that it would not fit the standard fenders. So special fenders, raked at the front and slightly shorter in length, were cast. Like the Daytona, the Super Bird (Plymouth's name for their Daytona clone) used retractable headlamps and a front chin spoiler. Rear-facing scoops mounted atop the front fenders were an appearance-only item, though on the real racer they vented the engine compartment. Black tape placed over and around the headlamp doors differentiated the Super Bird's nose from the Daytona's. A white Super Bird logo was placed on the left headlamp door. A special flat hood was used instead of the standard Road Runner's domed unit. Like the Daytona, the hood was held down at the front with two NASCAR-style hold down pins.

Large, colorful decals adorned each of the wing's vertical stabilizers.

The Charger's roofline allowed a smooth transition from the rear window to the rear deck lid. But the Road Runner's boxier shape did not allow for such a smooth transition. To make the rear window flush with the roof crown, a special convex rear backlight had to be used. To flow it smoothly into the lower body, a filler panel had to be welded in. Like the Daytona and the 1969 Charger 500s, Creative Industries performed the backlight conversions on the Super Birds.

Due to the aggressive production schedule, a black vinyl roof was made mandatory on all public-bought Super Birds. This way, instead of neatly finishing the rear window alterations, the rough spots could simply be hidden under the vinyl roof.

The Daytona had a coefficient drag of 0.29 while wind tunnel testing of the Super Bird showed a drag of 0.32. The Daytona was more slippery than the Super Bird because the Charger had been aerodynamically styled from its inception. The Super Bird's original drag numbers had been even higher, but the designers lowered the nose slightly to reduce the drag and give it a more normal look. Because of the design differences between the Charger and the Road Runner, the Super Bird had to use a more steeply raked rear wing.

Richard Petty's number 43 Plymouth had the name *Plymouth* spelled out across the rear quarter panels in

The Road Runner hardtop's interior was standard trim on the Super Bird.

white lettering. To give the public version that Petty look, Plymouth decals were placed on the Super Bird's rear quarters. Larger versions of the Super Bird logo were placed on the sides of the rear wing. This decal and the Plymouth decal were available in either white, for dark exterior colors, or black, for light colors. Exterior colors were limited to Blue Fire Metallic, Limelight, Vitamin C Orange, Deep Burnt Orange Metallic, Tor Red, Lemon Twist, Alpine White, and Petty Blue. There were no factory-painted black or red Super Bird's. Most Super Birds are white because that was the color with which they were first introduced.

Inside was the standard Road Runner hardtop interior in either all black or white/black combinations. Bench seats were standard and bucket sets were optional. The headliner was black regardless of the interior color. As with the Daytona, several options were not available for the Super Bird, including: Air Grabber hood, air conditioning, rear seat speaker, light package, rear window defrost, hood stripes, sill moldings, headlamp delay, Sure-Grip differential, and trailer package. The Super Bird used the same instrumentation as the 1970 Road Runner.

1970 GTX and Road Runner

"Men twenty-five and over take note" was how Plymouth worded the copy in the advertising for the 1970 GTX and its full-sized companion the Fury GT. These models were regarded as the executive branch of the rapid transit system. The ads targeted older adults by persuading them to buy GTXs instead of the "ignominious conveyances known as the family sedan." The target was the young married man with one or two kids who was being swayed to trade in his old car for a family sedan but still wanted to have the muscle car's power. The ad emphasized the luxury-car interior while downplaying the engine's power. The ad did not even mention the Hemi or the 440 six-pack options. Targeted marketing and low sales caused the removal of the convertible from the GTX series. Marketing reports revealed that a ragtop was hardly ever considered a family car.

Road Runners were targeted at the youth market, namely sixteen- to twenty-four-year-olds. Here, the emphasis

was on power and models' race-bred looks. Right away the ad emphasized the 383 engine with the 440 heads or the 440 with the three two barrel Holleys. Interestingly, the Hemi, which was losing market appeal, was not emphasized even to this young target audience. The Hemi now used a hydraulic cam so that owners were relieved from constantly adjusting the valves (a common complaint). Chrysler stressed the significance of the other powerplants. Those that wanted the Hemi knew it was available.

Changes to the Plymouth B-bodys included a revamped nose with a B-shaped grille. The GTX used a honeycomb textured insert while the Road Runner used multiple thin, vertical blades. As in previous years, the GTX nameplate was placed at the grille's center. For the first time, the Road Runner wore the Plymouth name on the left-hand side of the grille.

Front and rear views of the 1970 GTX. The two-door hardtop was the only body style available. Chrysler

The front bumper was also new and housed the front turn signal lamps which were now round. This was a direct copy of the Barracuda's lower-mounted Rallye lamps. The standard hood was one of the best-looking hoods to be placed on the second-generation B-bodies. It featured rear-facing, raised dome center section that looked similar to the cowl induction hood used on the Chevelle and Camaro, but it was non-functional. Engine call out badges were placed at the rear edge of the dome so that they could be read from the interior of the car, while decals placed alongside the dome told the outside world what was hiding beneath the steel bonnet. Cars with the 440 six-packs used decals that read "440+6." This engine

For 1970, the Road Runner remained Plymouth's leading muscle car.

Driver and passengers of a GTX or Road Runner knew exactly what was under the hood.

was available on the GTX, the Road Runner, and the Super Bird as optional equipment. Also listed as optional was the 426 Hemi, which wore decals that read "Hemi." Standard power on the Road Runner was still the 383ci 335hp V-8 and the standard power on the GTX and the Super Bird was the 440 Super Commando V-8. This engine was not optional in any other Road Runner.

The Air Grabber option continued, but it used one of the most unusual designs for air induction ever installed on a car. It was also sneaky. Air was forced down through a trapdoor that would pop up when the driver activated a switch on the instrument panel. Decals of teeth and the words "Air Grabber" were placed along the sides of the trapdoor and were visible when only when the scoop was raised. Without any outside graphics, a street racer could surprise their opponent at the line by raising the scoop.

Twin reflective stripes in either black, white, or gold were placed along the sides of the GTX as standard equipment; they could be deleted to provide a family car look. The stripes began at the forward edge of the front fender at the beltline and swept back across the door ending just in front of the restyled side air vents on the rear quarter panels.

The Road Runner's cartoon decal was moved from the door to the for-

ward section of the front fenders; it was the same decal, only a different location. A gold reflective tape stripe called a "dust trail" was optional and placed just above the beltline. It used a dust swirl pattern and a gold colored bird decal that replaced the one on the front fender. Like the GTX, the Road Runner name was mounted on the simulated air vents on the rear quarter panels. The Super Bird, however, did not use the Road Runner name, the bird decal, or the gold dust stripe.

The taillamps of both models were triangular and divided in the middle by a bezel. The GTX used a brightly trimmed bezel while the Road Runner and the Super Bird used a bezel painted the same color as the body, giving it a built-in look. The Plymouth name was spelled out below in bright lettering. The GTX used a bright trim piece just above the lettering that wraps down below the tail lamps. A small GTX emblem was placed on the right-hand edge of the deck lid. The Road Runner name was also spelled out here along with the bird decal. This setup was also used on the Super Bird. A decor group option added a tape stripe in either white, black, or gold. The stripe includes a colorful bird in a full speed run on the right-hand side of the deck lid.

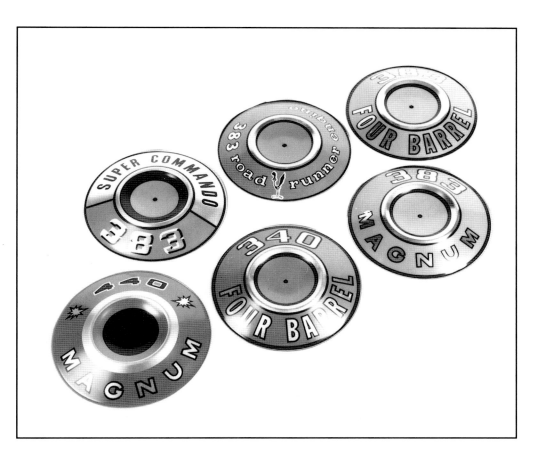

This "Beep Beep" is wearing a rear spoiler, an option made available for all models late in the year.

Colorful "pie tins" capped the air cleaners on all four-barrel V-8s. Year One

In 1970, all Plymouth muscle car B-bodys came standard with the Rallye instrumentation.

A performance hood option was available for all models except the Super Bird. The option consisted of a flat, black, wide center stripe placed over the center dome and flanked by two smaller outline stripes. As in years previous, this option was painted on; the stripes were not decals like the side stripes of the GTX model.

Chrysler reigned as king of the ovals in 1970. Between Dodge and Plymouth, Chrysler won all but ten races. Plymouth was racing two cars, both of which were teamed by Richard Petty. Petty himself drove number 43, and Pete Hamilton drove number 40. Plymouth won ten races, eight of the wins going to Petty and two to Hamilton. By the season close on November 20, 1970, Dodge had wrapped up the Manufacturers Championship.

On March 24, 1970, Buddy Baker broke the 200mph barrier while performing tire testing tires on his Dodge Daytona. On his thirtieth lap of the Talladega track, he was clocked at 200.096mph. The next time around, he broke his own record by reaching 200.336mph, followed by an outstanding 200.447mph. It was the first time a stock car had reached that speed on a closed course. It also earned the Dodge Daytona the title of the "World's Fastest Production Car."

Success often breeds contempt, and the Hemi-powered winged warriors were coming under attack by other drivers and manufacturers. One of the loudest cries was from General Motors, who had not won a single race in 1970. The best a GM driver had managed was Friday Hassler's fifth place finish in his 1969 Chevelle at the East Tennessee 200. Hassler was a full two laps behind Richard Petty's Plymouth and the second place Dodge. NASCAR officials agreed with Ford and General Motors that the winged cars provided "unfair competition." Their solution was to limit the Dodge and Plymouth cars to a 366ci engine displacement. "We protested the silly rule but it was no good," a Chrysler spokesperson said at the time. "They [NASCAR] claimed 'It was done to group up the pack so that one car would not run away from the rest and to make racing more exciting for the fans.' I guess we created the ultimate race car. One that was too good."

Even though Bobby Isaac won the championship in 1970, he lost his ride when Chrysler announced that they were cutting back for the upcoming 1971 season. In the future, they would have only two cars, both teamed by Richard Petty. One was the Plymouth driven by Petty himself and the other a Dodge Charger driven by Buddy Baker. And both would be driving all new designs.

Chapter 3

1971–1974

More Show Less Go

1971 Dodge

For 1971 the Coronet coupes and the Charger were blended into one model. Dodge's General Manager Bob McCurry remembered that it was decided to combine the two models so that two different floor pans could be used. In the past, designers had been locked into a predetermined design for the coupes because they shared the same floor pan with the four-door sedans. "With the two different floor pans," McCurry explained at the time, "we will be able to give the four-door buyer legroom almost equal to that of a full-sized car. And also [give] the hardtop enthusiast the sporty styling and appointments that they want." Because the Coronet name was most closely connected with the four-door family sedan and the Charger, regardless of its sub model, was regarded as more of a sporty car, it was decided that all 1971 mid-sized Dodge four doors would be Coronets and all mid-sized Dodge two doors would be called Chargers. Officially, however, the Charger was referred to as a two-door Coronet or fastback.

"I was fully involved with the Challenger and the Dart at that time," Bill

This 1972 Road Runner features some rare options, including the seldom seen colored-bumper group and the Air Grabber hood.

Brownlie said. He believed that the smaller high-performance cars, like the Demon 340, were the way to go. Mid-

When the Air Grabber option was added, horsepower increased.

sized muscle cars seemed to be on their way out—the victims of pressures from activists and insurance companies. So Brownlie turned the duties of restyling the new Charger line over to Diran Yajezian who saw life differently. Whereas Brownlie saw the Charger as a race car for the street, Yajezian wanted to take the Charger back to its roots. He wanted to make it more of a personal specialty car instead of the mid-sized street warrior that Brownlie had styled it for in 1968. His plan was to blend lines that were sporty enough for the muscle car buyer but not so outrageous that it would scare off an older buyer looking for a family car.

Many enthusiasts believe that this was the death of the Charger because it lost its unique styling. Brownlie, the man who created the classic Charger, agrees. "It varied too much away from the original concept. It no longer looked like a Charger," he said. "I did not like the design then and I still don't today."

The reality, however, was that Yajezian's design was right in line with that period of history. Brutal muscle cars were on their way out to be replaced by the mid-sized specialty car that Bouwkamp had first praised the 1966 Charger as being. It is doubtful that the powerful race-car-looking Charger could have survived. "Suddenly," Brownlie said, "high-performance

This Hemi-equipped 1971 Charger R/T was ordered with the colored bumper group.

Dodge's Ram Charger hood option was restyled for 1971 and operated like those on the 1970 Plymouth.

cars were no longer the thing to be selling. Government regulations were coming down hard on these cars. They wanted to make you build safer cars not faster cars." Yajezian's design created a whole new market for the Charger. In fact, this design outsold the original version.

Yajezian's design featured sleek lines with a slightly raked look. Although the lines were new, many of Brownlie's original styling cues survived to give the new Charger its sporty appearance. The front fenders narrowed slightly at the front to meet a chrome loop bumper which took its inspiration from the 1970 Charger and Coronet. Like the Charger it was a single loop; but like the Coronet it was divided in the middle. Also like the 1970 Coronet, the headlamps were exposed, which was a first for a production line Charger model. The decision to expose the headlamps was a simple issue. "It was just cheaper to expose the headlamps," said Brownlie. However, hideaway headlamps, which were optional on the other models, were made standard on the Special Edition so that it would have a distinct look from all the other Chargers.

Rectangular front turn signals mounted in the front pan. Two different hood styles were used. All models except the performance models. The Super Bee and Charger R/T used a flat hood with a single center crease line. Charger R/Ts and Super Bees used a domed hood The Super Bees used a center hood ornament that featured side indentions with louvers in the middle. A red engine call out was placed in the indentions of the flat black ornament. The Charger R/T used a louvered center and the engine call outs were placed alongside the dome portion of the hood.

The Ram Charger hood was optional and standard with the Hemi. It was restyled and used a trapdoor like the 1970 Plymouths. Front fender and rear quarter panel side lamps were rectangular shaped and divided by body color bezels. The Charger's body sides were clean and free of chrome just like its ancestors.

The influence of the E-bodies' Coke bottle styling could be seen in the doors and their nearly flush fitting outside handles. The roofline swept back using a semi-fastback design with a flush fit-

95

Special taillamps were standard on the Charger R/T models. They were also used with the colored-bumper group.

ting, contoured backlight. The rear deck lid was wide and sloped downward, creating a narrowing at the rear of the car and the look of a built-in rear lip spoiler (another of Brownlie's influences retained from the second-generation design).

Two different taillamp styles were used. Except for the Charger R/T, all were standard with twin red rectangular shaped lenses on each side separated in the center by a backup lamp. The Charger R/T used a one-piece lens that was divided into three separate units

Interior of the third generation Charger placed more emphasis on comfort but was still sporty.

on each side by a silver bezel. The bezel gave the appearance of deeply inset taillamps set at a right angle. Backup lamps were mounted on the inboard side of each set of taillamps. These same lenses were also used with the colored bumper group option.

The colored bumper group was available as an option on the Charger R/T and Super Bee models only with the standard exposed headlamps. With this option, the front and rear bumper were covered with body colored urethane plastic. This technology was first used by Chrysler as an option on the 1970 Plymouth 'Cuda models. Plymouth had borrowed the idea from Oldsmobile, who in turn was trying to copy Pontiac's GTO front styling of urethane plastic but without the expense. The process involved spraying an unchromed bumper with urethane foam then painting it the same color as

the rest of the car. The Charger's bumper group was available only with a few select colors, including Bright Blue, Citron Yella, Hemi Orange, Go Green, Plum Crazy, and Dark Green.

The interior is where the Charger models differed the most and where the Charger was distinguished from the two-door Coronet. The base Charger model, for all purposes, was the continuation of the Coronet two-door coupe but done in a drab flavor. An all-vinyl front bench seat was standard, and the instrument panel was an exact copy of the four-door sedans. Rectangular-shaped instrumentation dominated the dashboard's center with a 120mph speedometer housed in a deep, hooded instrument panel pad. No tachometer was optional with this instrument panel. However, a clock was optional and was positioned to the far right-hand side of the panel when ordered.

1971 Charger: A Coronet in Charger Clothing

The entry level Charger, like the 1970 Coronet coupe, came in two body styles: either a coupe with fixed rear quarter windows or a two-door hardtop. It was the only model where the fixed quarter window body style was available.

Charger coupe was the budget beater with a base list price of $2,707 and included as standard equipment a 225ci slant six-cylinder engine; three-speed manual transmission with column-mounted shift lever; three-spoke color-keyed steering wheel; heater/defroster; two-speed concealed wipers; dome lamp; and rubber floor mats. The Charger hardtop was priced slightly higher at just under $3,000 and included all of the coupe's standard features with these additions or changes: rubber floor mats were replaced with color-

Because Dodge considered the base Charger a Coronet, the Charger 500 was considered the first true Charger model. Chrysler

keyed carpeting and woodgrain inserts were added to the doors and instrument panel. A 318ci 230hp V-8 was optional in both body styles. Also optional was the 383ci V-8 with either two- or four-barrel carburetion.

Mid year saw another model placed between the coupe and hardtop. Called the Charger Topper, it was billed as the lowest priced Charger hardtop. This car was special because it came standard with a landau vinyl roof that covered only the forward part of the roof, white sidewall tires, full wheel covers, bumper guards, left remote control mirror, and bright finishing moldings.

The Charger script was placed on the rearward section of the front fend-

The Super Bee was based on the Charger for the last time in 1971. Chrysler

The performance hood of the 1971 Charger Super Bee wore this elaborate decal. Chrysler

ers and the Dodge nameplate was placed on the grille on the driver's side. The only outside identification used was a small emblem with the Charger's name and under it a "Dodge Division" ID plate. On the instrument panel above the glovebox was the word "Charger."

Next was the Charger 500 model, which returned for its final year of production. This model came in only one body style, the two-door hardtop, and was regarded as the first "true Charger model." As in 1970, the car was targeted for the buyer who wanted sporty looks but not the muscle of the muscle car. It was listed as "the sporty Charger" in the sales flyer.

Standard equipment included all that was on the Charger hardtop plus the 318ci V-8 for motivation. Inside were front bucket seats done in sculpted vinyl and a simulated walnut grain three-spoke steering wheel color keyed to the interior. The instrument panel was completely different from lower line Chargers. Instead of the long rectangular look, this Charger model used hooded round gauges including a 150mph speedometer, oil pressure and fuel gauges, and temperature and alternator gauges. Standard interior lighting included map and ash tray lamps. The reason the base Charger used the Coronet's instrument group was a pure marketing gimmick. The Charger 500's hooded gauges and 150mph speedometer echoed the muscle car image of the past, an attempt to distant the 500 from the family-targeted base model Chargers.

The front fender Charger script was also used on this model followed by the "500" emblem. A matching "500" emblem was also used on the rear deck lid. The "Dodge" nameplate was not used on the grille of this model. Colored vinyl body side moldings were also standard as were full wheel covers. Engine options were the same as those offered for the rest of the Charger line.

1971 Super Bee: The Great Contender

"And in this corner . . . " is the way the ad began in the 1971 Super Bee sales brochure. Since the Coronet two door was not officially available, the Super Bee was moved to the Charger line. But like the base Charger models, this model was also considered a Coronet because, like its ancestors, it was based on the low-ball Charger model. Only the hardtop body style was used; no Charger Super Bee coupes were built.

The overall concept was the result of the same pondering that went into the 1968 model. It was high on power and low on added accessories. Mechanically, it was the same in 1970, with the 383ci four-barrel Magnum V-8 standard. However, due to the fact that the engine was required to run on regular gasoline, the compression was dropped. It was now listed as 8.50:1 (in 1970 it had been 9.50:1), which lowered the horsepower output to 300hp at 4800 rpm. This engine was such a great performer that the 383 four barrel was deleted and the 383 Magnum took its place. The bad news was that it was no longer unique to the Super Bee; it could be ordered for all Charger models except the Charger R/T.

As in 1970, the standard transmission was a three-speed manual with a floor-mounted shift lever. Inside, the same platform that was used in 1968 was again used. The front seat was from the low-ball Charger hardtop and the instrument panel was the Charger 500's. Above the glovebox door on the instrument panel was the word "Super Bee."

On the front fenders, the Charger script was replaced with the "Super Bee" nameplate and a small bumble bee decal. A "Dodge" nameplate appeared on the grille. On the hood was the round Super Bee logo that had been used on the rear quarter panels in previous years. That decal was outlined with flat black accent striping on top of the center domed hood. On the deck lid, a bumble bee decal followed the Charger emblem.

Diran Yajezian hated the bumble bee stripes and devised a new way of striping the car. The stripes covered the center of the hood dome, divided and traced along the rear edge of the hood, then followed each side of the car along the upper contour lines to the car's rear. These stripes, as in previous years with the bumble bee stripes, were standard but could be deleted. The stripes were available in flat black only; no other colors were used even on black cars.

Engine options for the Super Bee were the same as in 1970, which included the 440 six-pack and the 426 Hemi. A mid-year powertrain option was available just for the Super Bee: the 340ci Magnum V-8 rated at 275hp at 5000rpm. The factory never officially offered the 440 four-barrel V-8 in the Super Bee, but a few are believed to have escaped.

1971 Charger SE: The Best Seller

Dodge's biggest selling Charger model was the highly trimmed Charger

Hideaway headlamps were standard on the Charger SE model and optional on other models. Chrysler

SE model. This had also been true in 1970, when nearly all Charger 500 and R/T models were ordered with the optional SE package.

The new Charger SE featured many of the same standard accessories found on the package in 1970, with some exceptions. Instead of bucket seats, a cloth and vinyl split-back bench seat with center arm rest was standard. Leather bucket seats were optional. Chrome trim around the pedals was again part of the SE package as was a lamp delay switch (a small green lamp above the ignition key switch that remained on for a few seconds after the driver closed the door). An ignition lock was also standard. The grille used with the concealed headlamps made it impossible to reach the standard hood release, hence an inside hood release was fitted to the SE model. A vinyl landau roof in either black, white, green, or gold was also standard.

Special SE emblems were placed on the C-pillars; similar ones were also placed inside the car on the instrument panel and the door panels. The Charger script was placed on the front fenders and the rear deck lid and followed by a Charger SE medallion.

The standard engine was the 318ci V-8, but powerplant options stretched all the way to the 440 Magnum V-8. Only the 440 six-pack and the Hemi were not available for the SE. Although a three-speed manual on the column was the standard transmission, over 95 percent of all Charger SEs were equipped with the automatic transmission; very few had the optional console.

1971 Charger R/T: One Last Snarl

The Charger R/T, like the Super Bee, made its last appearance in 1971. With a base list price of around $3,700, it was still the top model in the Charger family. Its standard equipment included all of the Charger 500 accessories plus the 440ci Magnum V-8 engine and a column-shifted automatic transmission. A floor-shifted four-speed manual gearbox was a no-cost option.

Other standard features included the louvered dome hood with flat black accent paint and an R/T logo decal on the hood's forward edge. The Charger script graced the front fenders followed by the red-and-black "R/T" emblem. An "R/T" emblem also followed the "Charger Dodge Division" nameplate on the deck lid's right-hand side. The Charger R/T's front doors were not used on any other Charger model. They featured two depressions accented with tape stripes.

Body side horizontal stripes, like those on the Super Bee, were also standard on the Charger R/T. Like the Super Bee, they could be deleted and were available only in flat black.

The standard heavy-duty suspension was a carbon copy of that used in previous models and included heavy-duty police drum brakes as standard equipment. Power front disc brakes were a popular option on all Charger models. Standard tires on the Charger R/Ts and Super Bees were G70x14in with raised, white lettering. Stamped steel wheels were standard and styled steel wheels were optional. Three styles of optional wheels were available: the chrome 14in road wheels that had debuted in 1967, and the slotted silver

Body stripes like these were standard on the R/T and Super Bee models.

A colorful bird's head was placed in the center of the 1971 Road Runner's grille. Chrysler

road Rallye wheel which had debuted in 1970. The latter were available in either 14x6in or 15x7in sizes. The 15in wheels came with G60x15in white-letter tires.

Several options were available for the Charger lineup, but not all were available for all models. The colored bumper group, front and rear spoilers, and body-colored racing mirrors were available only on the Charger R/T and Super Bee models. Air conditioning was available for all models except those with 440 six-pack or Hemi engines. The circle gauge cluster was optional in the base Charger coupe and hardtop.

A tachometer was optional with all models with the circle gauge cluster. When specified, it revised the gauge

layout. The fuel level and oil pressure gauges were moved to the right into a single, smaller gauge, and the water temp and ammeter were housed in another smaller gauge pod. This same arrangement was also used if the clock was ordered (the clock was not available if the tachometer was ordered).

Although the new design was 3in shorter in overall length than the 1970 Charger, the 1971 model looked longer because of the shorter 115in wheelbase. Yajezian's Charger is just under 1in narrower than Brownlie's classic version. While the 1968–1970 Charger had the feeling of race car to its interior, the 1971 felt more subdued and relaxing. The 1971 Charger SE model offered more hip room (58.5in) and had the feel of a well-crafted personal luxury car (such as a Thunderbird).

Many considered the Charger to be the best designed car of 1971, and *Cars* magazine.crowned it the "Top Perfor-

Next page
The 1971–1974 Plymouth B-bodys are one of designer John Herlitz's favorites.

mance Car of the Year." On the NASCAR ovals, Bobby Isaac won two races (the Firecracker 400 at Daytona Beach and the "Old Dominion 500" at Martinsville, Virginia) in his K &K insurance 1971 Dodge Charger. It would be the only two races a Charger would win this year.

1971 Plymouth: The Grand Champion

In 1971, the Belvedere name was dropped from the mid-sized Plymouths. Now, all four-door models were referred to as Satellites, while the two-door models were referred to as Satellite Sebrings. The name change provided the kind of separation the Dodge Coronet and the Charger models had. The Road

In a nod to 1968, engine call outs were placed on the sides of the simulated hood vents.

The Plymouth's lines were softer and rounder than the Charger's.

Runner and the GTX models returned and were based on the two-door Sebring models.

Unlike the Charger, there was only one body style available on the Road Runner and GTX models this year: a two-door hardtop. No coupes with fixed rear quarter windows were made.

John Herlitz was the Plymouth stylist most responsible for the new Satellite and Sebring's design, and it remains one of his favorites even over the 1970–1974 Barracuda. Herlitz worked hand in hand with Yajezian because major components between the Charger and the Road Runner would be shared. This was done to trim production costs. Herlitz and Yajezian used the same interior trim, seats, and instrumentation. However, Herlitz wanted the Plymouth to have its own identity on the outside, even more so than in previous years. The 1968–1970 Satellite models had looked very much like the Dodge Coronet models.

GM's newly restyled A-bodys demanded that Plymouth update their B-bodies to compete. As Yajezian had done with the Charger, the Plymouth now used a lower cowl height to give it that race car look. The four-door version of both models used a higher cowl position.

Because he didn't have to comply with a sedan's tight lines, Herlitz could allow his imagination to run free. He wanted a design that blended the sportiness of the Charger's lines while reducing the sharpness. Herlitz began his design at the roof and worked down, the opposite of Yajezian's, who styled from the wheels up. The roof's crown design combined with a more steeply angled windshield so smoothed the airflow over the car that the driver and passenger could drive with the windows down and not suffer the deafening wind noise experienced in other models. This design also proved beneficial in racing.

The Plymouth's front end tapered like that of the Charger but to a greater degree. Herlitz, who had created the front ends of the 1970 GTX and Road Runner, took those designs a step further in 1971 with a B-shaped, chrome, front bumper. For the first time since its introduction in 1968, the Road Runner used the same grille as on the GTX. Chrome bumpers were standard and colored bumpers were available as an option on both models, though few buyers opted for the colored ones. Large,

round, signal lamps were positioned in the front pan below the bumper.

To give the front end a uniform look, the hood was shortened and a filler panel filled the gap between the hood's leading edge and the grille. This gave the car a smoother, more aerodynamic look. The standard hood harked back to 1968, with two simulated air intakes and engine call outs placed along the outward sides.

On the GTX, thin horizontal lines (called hash marks) were placed inside the indentations. From a distance, these lines looked like vents. The idea behind the lines was to give the GTX a more upscale look than the Road Runner, which had no hood markings. An optional set of stripes for the GTX replaced the hash marks and flowed from the hood vents out over the front fenders. This set was available only with the standard hood.

The hood's rear edge rose upward to conceal the wipers. The raised lip was also carried over to the rear edge of the front fenders. Side lamps were less tall than those used on the Charger and were covered with a bezel that divided the lenses into three parts.

The GTX and Road Runner models, unlike the Charger, made a smooth transition from vertical to horizontal body contours. The fenders, doors, and rear quarter panels flowed gently into the lower sill of the car. Fender flares were placed over each opening and were tied together by a character line that cut across the doors' lower portion.

At the rear, the contours of the body graduated into a single loop bumper. The taillights were rectangular and divided by trim into four red lenses; backup lamps were integrated into the center of each housing. The deck lid was smooth and well rounded from the end of the backlight to the top of the rear bumper. The Road Runner decal on the deck lid featured a circle with the cartoon character in the center. The GTX used a "GTX" decal.

Other identification included GTX emblems mounted low, just in front of the rear wheelwell openings on the rear quarter panels. Road Runners wore the Road Runner nameplate and a cartoon decal just above the rear wheel opening.

Optional transverse stripes wrapped over the roof and down the sides of the rear quarter panels. These stripes were the work of Dick Samsen, who also designed the GTX's stripes. His objective with both sets of stripes was to emphasize the wheel openings. Stripes were available in black, white, or gold. If the transverse rear quarter stripes were ordered, the decal and emblems were removed and the stripe took their place.

A colorful bird's head graced the Road Runner's grille, and a "GTX" emblem that car's grille. For both models, the Plymouth medallion was placed in a depression in the center of the hood filler panel and surrounded by a round decal with the Plymouth name.

The Plymouth interiors included the same amenities as the higher trimmed Chargers, including a front bench seat and the same instrumentation. The Road Runner's standard steering wheel was a three-spoke, plastic rimmed item color-keyed to the interior. The GTX used a three-spoke steering wheel with soft touch buttons and simulated walnut trim.

Mechanically, the GTX was the same as the Charger R/T, and the Road Runner was the same as the Super Bee, including the 340ci V-8 option. The 440ci Super Commando V-8 was offered as an option for the Road Runner for the first time in 1971.

Other options for the Plymouths could usually be found on the Chargers as well, including front and rear spoilers and a center console. Two types of shift levers with the console: a pistol grip shifter for the four speed or the new slap stick. The slap stick featured a small T-shaped handle and was used with the automatic transmission. The slap stick had been designed with the performance driver in mind; it allowed the transmission to be shifted by bumping the lever and it would only go to one gear at a time. To shift into reverse or park, the driver pressed a small chrome button on the T's side.

The Air Grabber hood was again available, and for the first time it bore no resemblance to the standard hood. The Air Grabber featured a raised dome area with a cutout in the middle that housed the trapdoor. Flat black paint was used on the dome portion of the hood and the words "Air Grabber" appeared on the trapdoor. Engine call-

Plymouth shared the Charger's seat trim and instrument panel.

out decals, in either black or white, were placed on the front fenders. GTX transverse stripes were not available with the ram air hood.

Externally, the Plymouths were 2.2in shorter than the Chargers, although they both used a 115in wheelbase. The Plymouth was also a fraction of an inch taller than the Dodge, but both were the same width.

The Charger received more acclaim for its design than the Plymouth. But pretty faces don't count for much on the NASCAR oval and, here, the Plymouth

Now rated at 370hp, the 440 Super Commando became optional for the first time in a Road Runner.

1971 marked the last year Richard Petty would drive a Plymouth. That year he won twenty-one races and the first ever Winston Cup Championship. Chrysler

was dominant. Richard Petty drove his Plymouth stock car to twenty-one wins in 1971, allowing him to take the first ever Winston Cup Championship. He earned the Manufacturers Championship for Plymouth as well.

1972: Only the Memory Remains

By 1972, all of the true traits of the legendary muscle cars were gone, including most of the model names. The only survivor was the Plymouth Road Runner. The tide had turned against performance. "Performance looks" replaced real performance. The powerful engine was quickly becoming a relic.

Pete Hamilton won only one race in 1971, just inching out A.J. Foyt to win one of the qualifying rounds for the Daytona 500. Hamilton would finish in the top ten, twelve times that year. Chrysler

Two of 1972's biggest casualties were the 426 Hemi and the 440 six-pack. Although the 440 six-pack was listed as an option for the newest Charger model, the Rallye, and the Plymouth Road Runner, the big displacement engine was canceled just after the start of production. Only two 1972 Charger Rallyes and one Road Runner were built with the 440 six-pack option.

Emphasis on the look rather than the engine began in 1970 with the Charger 500, and was articulated in 1971 by Plymouth's Gordon Cherry: "There is more to a muscle car than its engine." Cherry felt, as did other product planners, that muscle car buyers were as motivated to buy by the look as actual performance.

The hottest option packages were not powerful engines, but the tape stripes and decals. Consider the 1971

Road Runner: most had only the standard powerplant and nearly all had the "C-Pillar" stripes. "Insurance companies were focusing on the engine and not the model," Cherry said. This was the driving force behind the movement to make smaller, less powerful engines standard.

1972 Charger: Rallye Is the Word

In 1972, the Dodge Charger lost the Super Bee and the Charger R/T, two of its hottest-selling model names. The decision was a simple one—lack of sales. The two models combined sold fewer than 7,000 units, while the Charger 500 moved better than 10,000 units. Despite the Charger 500's new emphasis on luxury over performance, its name was still closely tied to the race bred 1969 model in the minds of insurance companies. Rates were adjusted

The owner of this Road Runner wanted to see what the 440 six-pack V-8 option would have looked like in 1972, so he built one. Reportedly only one true 440 six-pack V-8 Plymouth was built. Note the engine block's color.

up just because of the earlier model's reputation.

Dodge wanted a model offering a high-performance look, without the high-performance engine. The product planning team's answer was the Charger Rallye option. This package could be ordered on the base Charger Coupe or Hardtop models and included all the trim necessary to make it look like a muscle car: the dome hood with black-out tape stripe; dark-colored, sculpted grille with horizontal slats; scalloped doors; and multi-louvered taillamps (a

direct carryover from the Charger R/T model).

Standard powerplant was that old Chrysler workhorse, the 318ci two-barrel V-8 rated at 150hp at 4000rpm. The 318 was also standard on the Charger SE, all other models were standard with the 225ci six-cylinder. Optional powerplants included an enlarged version of the 383, which now measured 400ci, in either two- or four-barrel form. All engines were optional in all Charger models. The 340ci four-barrel V-8 continued to be offered but only on Chargers with the Rallye option package. The 440ci four-barrel, now rated at 280hp, was optional only in the Charger SE or Chargers with the Rallye package.

Although the Charger Rallye lacked true muscle, it did have the necessary suspension equipment for straightening curves. In fact, it handled much better than even the previous Charger R/T offerings. The undercarriage equipment included the Rallye

suspension, heavy-duty brakes, standard, white-lettered F70x14in tire mounted on 14x6in stamped steel wheels.

Inside, all Charger models were standard with high-back, vinyl, front bench seats. The Charger Coupe came in three standard colors: black, blue, or green. The hardtop and Charger SE models added gold, tan, and white to the three other colors as standard trim.

The instrument panel was the same as that used in 1971. Base Chargers used the rectangular shaped cluster, and the Charger SE and those Chargers with the Rallye package used the circle cluster with a 150mph speedometer. Bucket seats in blue, green, black, gold, or white were optional in the Charger SE or the Charger hardtop models. They were not available in the coupes.

The Charger SE sold over twice the number of Charger R/Ts and Super Bees sold in 1971, and continued strong in 1972, with only minor restyling. The hidden headlamps were carried over as standard on the SE, but were no longer available on other Chargers.

The most unique feature about the Charger SE model was its vinyl-cov-

ered formal roofline. The SE's taillamps were also unique to that model. They were thinner and covered with a bright bezel.

As on the 1971 SEs, the wreath was placed on the C-pillars along with the model name in script. All other Charger models placed the "Charger" script followed by the signature medallion on the C-pillars. On the Charger SE, a small Charger script was placed high up on the rear half of the front fenders. No script was used on the fenders of the other Charger models.

A Brougham option was available for the Charger SE. This package added a cloth and vinyl high back bench seat or all vinyl bucket seats and special medallions on the door panels and instrument panel.

Chargers were available in a total of eighteen exterior colors. The line-up included two extra cost, high impact colors: Hemi Orange and Top Banana. Other options included a sunroof, which was available with the vinyl roof only. Few Chargers were built with this option.

During the latter part of the model year, three specially priced packages were released as dealer incentives. One

The Charger SE utilized a special roofline. Chrysler

was the A07 package for the Charger SE. Included in this option package was nearly every option a driver might want, including power steering, power front disc brakes, automatic transmission, AM radio with rear seat speakers, variable speed wipers, air conditioning, dual chrome racing mirrors, whitewall tires, undercoating and hood insulator pads, light package (which included the lamp delay switch for the ignition key and headlamp-on buzzer). Also included was an electrical clock, tinted glass, bumper guards, rear defogger, and the Brougham package. This was one of the most well-equipped models Dodge had ever offered.

The Charger Topper package also returned and included the canopy vinyl roof, concealed headlamps, inside hood release, Rallye instrumentation, bumper guards, special hood deck bumper and sill moldings, and body side stripes. A Charger Topper X package also appeared and was a combination of the Charger A07 and the Topper package, including all of the Topper package and the A07 option except the Brougham package. All three models were released around the mid-year point and listed as marketing tools. The Topper and Topper X were available on the Charger hardtop models only.

Because Chrysler pulled out of racing in 1972, Richard Petty finally drove a Dodge Charger. He picked up STP as a sponsor and a new color—red—was added to the sides of his car. Petty said that of all of his race cars, the 1971–1974 Charger was his favorite, explaining that it handled even better than the winged Super Bird. Petty raced the Charger from 1972 to 1980 and captured the checkered flag thirty-seven times.

1972 Plymouth: Road Runner Stands Alone

Road Runner stood officially as the only mid-sized muscle car Plymouth offered in 1972. If a buyer ordered the 440ci V-8 engine, it came with the "GTX" logo on the deck lid and body sides and special accent striping. This appearance set up was also used if a buyer ordered the 440 six-barrel. It is reported that only one 440-6 was built.

Plymouth continued to use the body styling it had unveiled in 1971 with natural evolutionary changes. These included a vertical bezel that divided the grille into two openings. The taillamps were angled inward at the bottom, and the rear bumper was also revised to accommodate this change. Steve Bollinger was responsible for the changes in the car's taillamps and rear bumper.

For identification, the cartoon likeness and name were still placed on the rear quarter panels but they were positioned lower than in 1971. The bird's head was eliminated from the grille, but one was placed inside the circular emblem on the hood filler panel. The Road Runner nameplate was positioned on the lower left-hand side of the

111

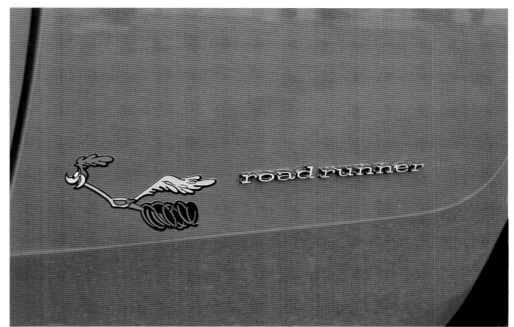

Roof strobe stripes and rear spoilers were carryovers from the 1971 model year.

Even when placed on a 1972 model, this name was a head-turner.

grille bezel. A circle-shaped decal of the bird was on the rear deck lid.

The hood continued with the same styling as in 1971. The C-pillar stripe returned, as did the front fender stripes (standard with the Road Runner/GTX model and available only with the standard hood). The C-stripe and fender stripes could not be ordered together.

Another stripe scheme was also available. It used one single center stripe on the hood and twin stripes on the deck lid. This stripe scheme was only available on Road Runners ordered with the Air Grabber hood. All stripes were available in either black or white.

Unlike the Charger Rallye, the 1972 Road Runner was standard with a big block 400ci four-barrel V-8. It was rated at 255hp at 4800rpm and 340lbs-ft of torque at 3200. In California, it was rated at 246hp at 4800rpm and 335lbs-ft of torque at 3200rpm. If the Air Grabber hood was ordered, the rating rose to 265hp and 345lbs-ft of torque. The Air Grabber hood was not available in a California.

The 340ci small block was again optional. This engine was rated at 240hp at 4800rpm and 290lbs-ft of torque at 3600rpm in all states. Al-

though it had less power than in 1971, it was a better running engine. The 1971 version suffered from lags in acceleration, especially from a standstill or when passing. But a new cam and a little fine tuning of the carburetor ended that bog.

For all Road Runners but those sold in California, the top of the line was the 440ci four-barrel V-8 rated at 280hp at 4800rpm and 375lbs-ft of torque at 3200rpm. Those in the Golden State were rated at 271hp at 4800rpm and 370lbs-ft of torque at 3200rpm. The Air Grabber hood increased output to 290hp at 4800rpm and 380lbs-ft of torque at 320 rpm, but this engine was not available in California either. A total of 672 Road Runner/GTXs were built with the 440ci powerplant. Over 2,000 were built with the 340ci V-8, supporting the new trend toward smaller engines.

The Road Runner's standard seating followed the original low-buck street racer concept and consisted of a low-grade vinyl bench seat with a higher grade interior in either bench seat or bucket seats as optional. Instrumentation was unchanged from 1971. Options included a clock or tachometer; the soft rim "Tuff" steering wheel; a vinyl top,

Now that the GTX was gone, the 1972 Road Runner's interior used more walnut trim.

available in black, green, gold, white, or tan; and either full or canopy tops. A power operated sunroof was a rare option and available only with the vinyl roof. As with the Charger, all engines except the 400 four-barrel came standard with electronic ignition (it was optional on the 400, and most dealers added it as a required option).

Road Runners still came standard with the Rallye type suspension, which now included a front and rear sway bar. This was the same setup used on the Charger Rallye package.

Plymouth spent over $50,000 to rework an old army vehicle horn to duplicate the "beep beep" sound of the Warner Brother's cartoon star. It was used in all 1968–1974 Road Runners.

As further testimony to the decline of high-performance, the long list of axle packages disappeared in 1972. The Track Pack was the sole survivor, but it was only available with the 440ci V-8/four-speed manual combination. The Track Pack was canceled shortly after production began, and it is unclear if any Charger or Road Runner was equipped with it. The Track Pack, like the 440ci six-pack, was a victim of ever-tightening emissions standards.

1973 Charger: Longer and Wider

The Charger line was Dodge's second best-selling model, just behind the Dart, and the SE was the best-selling model of the line. This can be attributed to subtle but important changes made to the 1973 Charger.

The biggest change went fairly unnoticed; the car grew by 7in in length (now 212.7in) and wider by a fraction of an inch (now 77in). Height remained

the same. Most of the length was in the longer rear quarter panels.

Other exterior changes included a new grille with a larger crosshatch pattern. The Charger SE used a slightly different grille that featured a horizontal bar across the center. The hidden headlamps, even as an option, were eliminated to cut the cost of the new design.

One of the new Charger SE's most striking design features was its new roof, which replaced the moveable quarter window with a fixed opera window. This marked the beginning of the Chevrolet Monte Carlo's influence on the Charger. To give the Charger a sportier look, the windows were covered with canted louvers that matched the standard half vinyl roof in color. Beginning November 1, 1972, another roofline became a no-cost option on the SE model. This roofline, called a Halo Roof, had moveable quarter windows and a vinyl roof, which did not extend as far down the sides. Both of these rooflines were limited to the Charger SE models only. Vinyl top colors were black, white, gold, or parchment.

At the Charger's rear were multi-louvered taillamps, each featuring eleven separate lenses. For identification, the Charger script was moved from the C-pillars to the leading edge of the front doors and followed by the signature medallion on all models except those Charger coupes and hardtops with the Charger Rallye package op-

tion. That option came with special body side stripes that included the model's name. The "Dodge" name was spelled out in bold capital letters on the left-hand side of the hood of all models.

The Charger SE also used some special identification markings, which included a wreath on the C-pillars. A similar wreath design was used on the hood as a stand-up ornament.

Dodge Division emblems were still used on the rear deck lid on the far right-hand side. Interior identification appeared on the instrument panel just above the glovebox door.

The Charger Rallye models were such a success in 1972 that they continued into 1973 largely unchanged. Solid colored body side stripes were added and graduated colored stripes were optional on the Rallye as well as all other Chargers.

Mechanically, the Charger was unchanged from 1972, but all powerplants were now standard with electronic ignition systems. Horsepower ratings tumbled even further.

The base Charger coupe and hardtop models were still standard with the 225ci six-cylinder, which was now rated at 105hp. The Charger SE and those with the Rallye package option came standard with the base 318ci V-8 which remained the same as in the previous year.

Optional engines included the 340ci V-8, but only for those cars with the Rallye package. Two versions of the

The best-selling Charger was the SE model.

400ci big block were still available for all Charger models: the two-barrel version was now rated at 185hp at 3600rpm and the four-barrel version was rated at 260hp at 4800rpm. The 440ci four-barrel V-8 was also available, but only for the SE and Rallye equipped models. The 440 lost its Magnum name and 10hp and was now rated at 280hp at 4800rpm. Torque, however, remained the same. Dual exhaust was standard on all models equipped with a four-barrel carbureted engine.

Charger options for 1973 included a sunroof with a full vinyl roof and a host of radio possibilities including AM, AM/FM, and AM/FM with cassette tape player. Power steering and power disc brakes were available for the hardtops and SEs only. A tachometer and clock were optional only on cars with the Rallye instrument cluster. Styled Road Wheels or slotted Rallye wheels were also optional. The standard transmission was a three-speed manual on all but the Charger SE. An automatic or four-speed manual with a Hurst shifter was optional.

Bucket seats were optional in all but the Charger coupe with the fixed rear quarter windows. A console was a no-cost option in the Charger SE if bucket seats were ordered; and a regular option on other models. Trim was in all vinyl except for a cloth and vinyl

Styled steel wheels were standard on the Road Runner models.

bench seat with a center arm rest that was optional in the Charger SE only.

1973 Road Runner: Are You or Aren't You?

"Are you or aren't you?" was the question posed on the catalog cover for the 1973 Plymouth line. This was a particularly good question to direct at the 1973 Road Runner—"Are you or aren't you" . . . a muscle car? Gone was the bird's standard big block 400ci V-8, replaced by the garden variety 318ci small block. Dual exhaust was the only modification that differentiated the Road Runner's 318 from that fitted to any other Plymouth. It marked the first time that a single two-barrel carburetor had powered the legendary model.

The 1973 Road Runner sported new looks both front and rear, and an overall length increased by more than 7in (now 210.8in). The previous year's hoop bumper was expensive to manufacture, so to decrease overall cost a conventional bumper design took its place. The new grille used a larger egg crate pattern with a center horizontal bar. The flat black grille was flanked on both sides by dual headlamps mounted in large, bright bezels. The front parking lamps were rectangular and mounted behind the grille.

The hood was also restyled and included a large, raised dome in the cen-

ter with twin simulated air intakes on the forward edge. Heavy feature lines were used on the hood and these were transferred to the front filler panel, which now sported a decal of the cartoon character instead of an emblem. The Air Grabber option was canceled shortly before the end of the 1972 production run, hence no 1973 Road Runners came with functional hood scoops.

At the back, the bumper was made beefier, and the taillamps were restyled similar to those used in 1971, but with only three divisions per lamp. The rear deck lid kept its rounded shape. The Road Runner decal was restyled such that the colorful bird was no longer placed in a circle.

The unattractive sport striping used in 1972 was replaced with revised C-pillar stripes. The new stripes—available in black, white, or red—ran over the top of the roof and along the upper body side contours, terminating at the leading edge of the front fender. The Road Runner insignia was placed in the stripes on the C-pillars. These stripes were standard, but could be deleted under option V88. Stripes in the same colors placed along the sides of the hood were optional but only if the standard stripes were retained.

In the 1960s, muscle cars had come to prominence on the strength of powerful engines. By 1973, however, looks were the most important. Since a popular option was the styled wheels, the Slotted Road Rallye Wheels were made standard. The older style chrome spoke road wheels remained optional, as did 15in Rallye wheels. Wheel covers of any kind were no longer available on any Road Runners. White lettered F70x 14in tires were also standard; whitewall tires were not available.

A total of sixteen exterior colors were available for the Road Runner and the interior came in three standard colors: blue, green, or black. The optional bench seat interior came in one of five colors: blue, green, black, parchment, or gold. Bucket seats were offered in these colors plus white.

A three-speed, synchromesh, manual transmission with a floor shift was standard with the 318ci or 400ci V-8, and the automatic was standard with the 440. A four-speed manual with a Hurst pistol grip shifter was optional with all but the 440ci V-8. The auto-

matic was available with all engine sizes. A suspension with front and rear sway bars and front disc brakes was standard.

1974: The Last Ride of Dodge's White Stallion

The Charger made one final last stand as a sporty car in 1974. All of the models returned, including the Rallye option package. The turning of the tide could be felt at Chrysler and was a warning of things to come.

In 1973, the Charger SE sold nearly 60,000 copies. This means that over 50 percent of the 1973 Chargers sold were SE models. As a result, the "luxury Charger" dominated the 1974 sales brochure. The Rallye, which was a distant third in sales, was so buried that few buyers knew it was available.

The Charger's overall length grew again and now measured 214in. This growth spurt was due largely to new bumpers required by a federally mandated 5mph crash test. The grille was the same as the year before as were all identification emblems and decals.

Hoping to further cash in on the personal-sized car market, Dodge offered a special Charger body shortly after the start of production. Called a Celebrity Roof, it was nothing more than the Charger SE's roofline with the louvered panels removed and the fixed opera window in full view. This option was coded as a vinyl top and listed as option code A07. It was available in the same color as the standard vinyl roof (white, black, gold, or parchment).

A special marketing option called the Charger Spring Special was introduced late in the model year. The special was painted in what Dodge called earth colors. Sienna Metallic (option code KT5) was standard. Black (TX9), Parchment (HL4), and Dark Moonstone (KL8) were optional colors. Regardless of the exterior color, the body side stripe (code V6K), which was part of the package, was parchment/brown (the colors graduated into each other). Vinyl side molding was available as a no-cost replacement option for the side stripes.

Inside, this special Charger package used a special cloth and vinyl bench seat with parchment, brown, and black stripes and dark brown carpeting. Neither bucket seats nor a floor-shifted

transmission were optional with this model . Other standard features included bumper revel moldings, wheel lip moldings, and the SE sound insulation package. A vinyl top or the celebrity roof was optional, but only in parchment or black. No separate production figures were maintained for the Spring Special because it was part of another option package listed as code A77. It is believed to be rare, as is the celebrity roof. It is believed that fewer than 1,000 units were made of each model.

Stripes of all shapes and colors were available for all Charger models. A rear deck stripe was available in black but only if it lapped over the deck lid's rear edge. The black hood stripe on the Rallye was now optional. Black side stripes continued to be standard with the Rally package, and graduated colored stripes were optional on all Charger models. Thin upper body side stripes in a host of colors were standard equipment on the Charger SE.

1974 Road Runner: A Fading Dream

The Plymouth Road Runner also received few changes in 1974. As with the Charger, new bumpers increased its overall length. Another change was engine call outs on the sides of the dome hood. Body side stripes were again standard and were the same pattern and style as the year before. Hood stripes were again optional, but they

too used cutouts that showed the engine displacement.

Engine options were the same as in 1973, with the 318ci V-8 with dual exhaust standard. The 400 four-barrel was optional except in California where it was not available. Both the 318ci and the 400ci engines were available with either four-speed manual or automatic transmissions. A three speed in the floor was standard, but the 440ci engine was available only with the automatic transmission. The big engine could not pass emissions requirements if the four-speed manual transmission was fitted.

Emission standards also took their toll on the 340ci engine, which did not return. Instead, the 340 grew to 360ci. Unlike the 340ci powerplant, the 360ci V-8 came in two versions: a single exhaust rated at 200hp, which was available in all models, and a dual exhaust version, which was available only in the Road Runner or Rallye Charger.

Regardless of the exhaust system fitted, a four-barrel carburetor was used. Engines sold in California carried mandatory additional emission controls and were limited to the single exhaust.

The 400ci V-8 was available in either two-barrel or four-barrel form, rated at 205hp and 250hp respectively. Dual exhaust was standard on all four-barrel-equipped models. The 440 four-barrel rated at 275hp and was optional

The 1974 Road Runner was unchanged from 1973.

in the Charger SE, Charger Rallye, and Road Runner models only.

A new option on the Plymouth Road Runner was chrome 15in wheels. The wheel was finished to look like cast aluminum and used a chrome center hub and lug nuts. This wheel was first used on the full-sized 1971 Furys, and it was added to the Plymouth mid-sized line in 1974. With this option, buyers got four styled wheels and a standard stamped steel spare wheel painted gloss black. With the standard 14in slotted Rallye wheels, the spare matched those on the car. Chrome, spoked, road wheels in 14in size made their last appearance this year. Like the 15in wheels, a stamped steel wheel was used as a spare tire.

The 1974 models underwent little change from 1973 because a shake-up in how Chrysler designed cars was taking place. No longer would the company be separated by division. Now, one team would design one car line, while another team would handle another line. Bill Brownlie chose to leave the intermediates and go to the smaller models because he believed these would be the most popular cars. Brownlie's departure would have a big effect on the mid-sized cars as the smaller cars would become the bases for future performance packages.

Chapter 4

1975-1979

The Epitaph

By 1975 the words *high-performance* had became a distant memory. The gas shortage caused a metamorphosis at all automobile manufacturing corporate headquarters. Suddenly, the buyer was no longer asking questions like "How much horsepower does it have?" or "How fast will it go?" Instead, they were asking "How many miles per gallon?" Muscle cars were truly no more.

Even used street brawlers of the 1960s and early 1970s were sent into a tailspin because of drastic turnarounds in the market. Suddenly, muscle cars went from the front of car lots, where they had always drawn big crowds, to the back rows. Nobody wanted one of these gas guzzlers and dealers knew it. Fine examples of America's automotive history were selling for a few hundred dollars. When I asked about the price of a 1968 Super Bee on one Chrysler lot, the dealer replied, "How much money do you have in your pockets?" That dealer had taken it in on a new car trade. The new car was a 1975 Charger.

The 1975 Charger, however, was nothing like the ultimate road and track car Bill Brownlie had first envi-

Based on the Dodge Aspen coupe, 1978's Super Coupe had the performance look but little more. This handsomely restored example belongs to Harold Samuels of Hershey, Pennsylvania.

sioned . While the 1971-1974 Charger was not the tough-looking street racer of 1968–1970, at least it was sporty. The new interval Charger couldn't manage even sporty .

In 1973, Chevrolet had brought out their sleek, stylish, Monte Carlo. At the same time Chrysler was intertwining all car lines. As a result, the 1975 Charger was to be designed by the same team that had designed the Coronet, Fury Sport, and the new Chrysler Cordoba. Bill Brownlie had left the mid-sized line and was now putting the

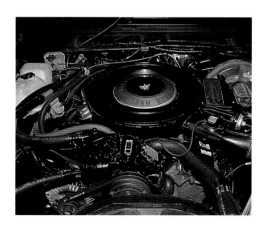

By the late-1970s a "muscle" car's engine had so many hoses and anti-pollution devices attached that it looked as if it were on a life support system. And maybe it was . . . certainly the performance was nearly dead.

finishing touches on the F-bodied Volare and Aspen models to be released the next year.

The mid-sized designers saw the success of the 1973 and 1974 Chevrolet Monte Carlo and decided to make the Charger into a competing model. In the process, they changed the Charger so much that it looked more like GM had styled it. The resemblance is truly uncanny. At the front were two single round headlamps deeply inset into the fenders with round turn lamps mounted on the outboard sides of the grille—just like the Chevrolet. The heavily sculpted hood and fixed opera windows in the roof pillars were also strongly reminiscent of the Monte. Burt Bouwkamp said that the opera windows "were recognition elements" in the specialty, personal-sized car market.

The design lines of the Charger and Cordoba were nearly identical. The lines of each were more square and straight than the flowing lines of the Monte Carlo. The Charger also seemed to sit lower than the Cordoba, as if it was chopped and channeled. Contours in the fenders and the quarter panels further echoed the Monte Carlo. GM styling cues could also be seen on the car's rear. While it looked nothing like the Monte Carlo, it did reflect on the Pontiac Grand Prix with large tail-lamps and a sharply designed deck lid.

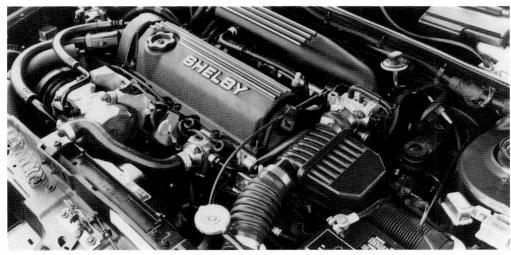

Part of the ad copy for the Super Coupe described it as "enough to moisten the eye of any veteran tough car fan." If you had driven a Hemi in the late-1960s and then had been offered this as a performance car ten years later, you'd cry, too.

Small cars became Chrysler's performance car base in the 1980s. The 1987 Shelby Charger featured a Shelby Automobiles-modified 2.2 liter four-cylinder. Turbocharging helped produce 175hp, propelling the car from 0–60mph in 6.95sec. Shelby Automobiles

Inside, the Charger was plush and soft with all vinyl front bucket seats and a center armrest. Cloth bucket seats with extra padding were optional and gave the Charger the feel of an expensive luxury car. The door panels were heavily padded and styled, again reminiscent of the Chevrolet. The instrumentation was ample but not very sporty with a round 120mph speedometer—the 150mph speedometer forever gone.

The standard power was a 360ci V-8 with a two-barrel carburetor rated at 180hp at 4000rpm. A 318ci V-8 rated at 145hp at 4000rpm was optional. Shortly after production, the 400ci V-8 became available in either a two-barrel rated at 175hp or a four-barrel rated at 190hp at 4200rpm. The four-barrel was the hottest engine available, as the 440ci V-8 was no longer available for the mid-sized models, except in police-optioned Coronet Sedans.

Dual exhaust was optional on the 400ci four-barrel, which raised the horsepower rating to 235. Because over 55 percent of all Chargers sold in 1974

In 1976, Dodge resurrected the Daytona name on a tape-striped and painted Charger. Shown here is a 1977 model. Chrysler

had been SE models, Dodge eliminated all other Charger models from the 1975 line-up.

Change was just as wide-sweeping for the once proud Road Runner. Its sleek styling died when the Satellite was discontinued as its base. When it returned for 1975, it found a home on the all new Fury Custom sport coupe, the model tapped to replace the Satellite. The same team that had designed the Charger and Cordoba also designed the Fury Custom and the Road Runner, and the overall look reflected it.

The Midnight Charger was a 1977 limited edition model. A total of 2,993 were built. The package included special grille and tail-lamp treatments, sport mirrors, and an elk grain, padded, landau top with opera window. Chrysler

The Road Runner's lines were straighter and less formal than the Charger's. At the front was a wide grille with a fine mesh covered by ten horizontal bars. The signal lamps were mounted behind the grille. The grille was flanked by single round headlamps trimmed by bright bezels. For the first time, the Road Runner used no special hood. Body side stripes passing up and over the roof were again standard as were G70x14in white letter tires mounted on Road Rallye wheels. Slotted chrome road wheels were optional as were new polycast urethane wheels painted to match the body.

Power came from a standard 318ci V-8. Unlike the 1974 models, no 440 four-barrel was available. The largest and most powerful engine was the 400ci four-barrel V-8 rated at 190hp at 400 rpm and 290lbs-ft of torque at 3200rpm. Inside, a vinyl bench seat was standard and bucket seats were optional. Instrumentation was the same as the Charger. Car testers were distinctly underwhelmed. In a review of the 1975 Road Runner, *Car and Driver* wrote that "a Road Runner without acceleration is just another Plymouth."

In 1976, Dodge, hoping to revive some of the old excitement, dusted off the Daytona name and pasted it onto a two-toned Dodge Charger SE They also introduced the Charger and Charger Sport, which were the 1975 Coronet two doors once again blended into the Charger line.

The Road Runner saw a big change in 1976 when it became on option package on the smaller Volare. It would remain on this platform until its demise in 1980. Bill Brownlie came up with an idea he called "son of Road Runner" based on a small sporty car with a turbocharged engine, competition four wheel drive suspension, and a full array of outside air dams and spoilers. Plymouth said no thanks.

The 1977 Charger remained basically unchanged from the 1975 version. The Daytona returned, this time using a two-tone decal treatment. Dodge also offered a limited edition Charger called the Midnight Charger Special. This model used a special plastic front end with slotted divider bars across the grille that were painted the same color as the body. A rich leather interior was standard, as were body-colored racing mirrors, road wheels, and a landau top. This year also saw the newly restyled Monaco take the base Charger and Charger Sport's place leaving the Charger SE as the only model. The Daytona and Midnight Special were considered package options on the SE. A new option introduced late in 1977

Last of the performance Dodge B-bodys was the 1979 Magnum XE, which replaced the Charger. Chrysler

was a T-bar roof that featured two removable roof panels.

The Charger returned for the last time as a mid-sized model in 1978 along with a sporty offshoot model called Magnum XE. The Magnum XE used the Charger's basic body shell, but sported a rounder, sportier nose with plastic covers over the four rectangular headlamps.

A Grand Touring option (Code A75) called Magnum GT was also offered. It included color-keyed polycast urethane 15x7in wheels with GR60x 15in white letter tires and a performance suspension with heavy-duty shock absorbers. Also standard were a machine-turned instrument panel and a two-spoke leather steering wheel connected to a quick-ratio power steering gearbox. The Magnum GT was available in only seven colors. Standard colors were Classic Cream, Eggshell White, Bright Canyon Red, and Black. Extra cost colors were Pewter Grey, Starlight Blue Sunfire, and Tapestry Red Sunfire.

Engine options were the same as for the Charger, and included a 318ci Lean Burn V-8 rated at 140hp. The

123

The 1978 Magnum XE was Dodge's last-ditch effort at a mid-sized muscle car. Chrysler

most powerful engine was a 400ci four-barrel. Overall, the Magnum outsold the Charger, and the Magnum XE outsold the Magnum GT, which accounted for less than 2 percent of total Magnum sales.

For 1979 the Magnum XE and the Magnum GT returned, but the Charger was left to rest in peace. Chrysler revised the 300 nameplate and placed it on a specially trimmed Cordoba. It featured the trademark crosshatch bar grille and 300 identification, rear quarter windows, and standard road wheel center caps. Other trim included front fender louvers and distinctive red, white, and blue body side and deck stripes.

The 300 was powered by a 360ci four-barrel V-8 rated at 195hp at 4000rpm. A handling package with front and rear sway bars was also standard. It was available in Spinmaker White only with a red leather interior, front bucket seats, and machine-turned instrument panel.

Only 3,811 300 option packages were installed on the 1979 Cordoba,

which accounts for a mere 5 percent of the total Cordoba production.

Except for new taillamps, the Magnum was the same as in 1978. The 318ci V-8, now rated at 135hp, was again the standard engine. Gone was the big block 400ci V-8; now the most powerful engine was a 360ci HO V-8 four-barrel rated at 195hp at 4000rpm. Magnum sales fell to about half of that sold in 1978, so Dodge canceled it.

The beginning of the new decade brought a new Chrysler. The popular selling models were small front wheel drive cars powered by small transverse mounted four-cylinder powerplants. The sales total of the 1980 Omni/Horizon line was 250,000 units. It was clear that the buying public wanted small, fuel efficient cars and that the days of the 440ci power muscle cars would never return.

Cars with a sporty feel were still sold in 1980, and the newest model, the Mirada, took the place of the departed Magnum XE. The Mirada featured a soft, highly-angled front facia with single headlamps.

Two models were offered: the base and Mirada S. A sporty CMX package was offered for both models. It included color-keyed bumpers, accent moldings, and body side stripes and special badges. A total of 5,384 Miradas were

equipped with this package, most on the base model. Another special option was the Cabriolet vinyl top, which simulated the look of a convertible top. A total of 936 Miradas wore this option, of which only seven were Mirada Ss.

Only the Mirada S would return in 1981. The CMX package expanded to include the Cabriolet top. A total of 1,683 Miradas were outfitted with this package. The Mirada continued basically unchanged through 1983, its last year of production.

Late in 1982, the tide turned again towards high-performance but this time for the smaller cars. Dodge offered a "Charger" option on the Omni hatchback which included decals, a hood scoop, and spoilers. It was so popular with buyers that it returned the next year as its own model. Late in the year, Carroll Shelby would give the package real performance.

With the assistance of a turbocharger, Shelby squeezed 146hp at 5200rpm out of a 136ci four-cylinder. It was a good performer, but never really lived up to its name. It was deleted in 1987.

Chrysler may not have become fully involved in the muscle car wars in the early years (1964–1966), but they came in hard and fast offering the most mid-sized muscle cars (Dodge offered three and Plymouth two) and the biggest and most powerful base powerplant (the high performance 440ci V-8 with 375hp).

And of course there was the Hemi.

No other engine has had such a dominant influence on racing. Whether it was at the drag strip or around a NASCAR oval, a Chrysler was always a safe bet. The late 1960s—early 1970s was an entirely different time. Those who experienced it recall that you didn't challenge a mid-sized Dodge or Plymouth that sounded like a coffee can full of rocks. For that sound meant Mopar and that meant Hemi.

So if some dark night you happen to hear that distinctive clatter and rumble next to you at a lonely stoplight, you better look quick. Because when the light changes your neighbor will be gone in a Hemi flash.

Appendix A

Production Totals

Model	Body Style	Total Units	Model Total	Model	Body Style	Total Units	Model Total
1966				Road Runner	coupe	32,717	
Charger	fastback	37,344	37,344	Road Runner	hardtop	47,365	
				Road Runner	convertible	2,027	82,109
1967							
Charger	fastback	14,980	14,980	**1970**			
Coronet R/T	hardtop	9,553		Charger	fastback	9,374	
Coronet R/t	convertible	628	10,181	Charger 500	fastback	27,432	
GTX	hardtop	11,429		Charger R/T	fastback	9,509	46,315
GTX	convertible	686	12,115	Coronet R/T	hardtop	2,172	
				Coronet R/T	convertible	236	2,408
1968				Super Bee	coupe	3,640	
Charger	fastback	74,925		Super Bee	hardtop	10,614	14,254
Charger R/T	fastback	17,665	92,590	GTX	hardtop	7,202	7,202
Coronet R/T	hardtop	9,989		Road Runner	coupe	14,744	
Coronet R/T	convertible	569	10,558	Road Runner	hardtop	20,899	
Super Bee	coupe	7,842	7,842	Road Runner	convertible	684	
GTX	hardtop	17,246		Super Bird	fast top	1,935	38,262
GTX	convertible	1,026	18,272				
Road Runner	coupe	29,240		**1971**			
Road Runner	hardtop	15,358	44,598	Charger	coupe	471	
				Charger	hardtop	41,564	
1969				Charger 500	hardtop	10,306	
Charger	fastback	65,429		Charger SE	hardtop	14,641	
Charger R/T	fastback	19,298		Super Bee	hardtop	4,144	
Charger 500	fast top	450*		Charger R/T	hardtop	2,659	73,785
Daytona	fast top	503	85,680	GTX	hardtop	2,626	2,626
Coronet R/T	hardtop	6,518		Road Runner	hardtop	13,046	13,046
Coronet R/T	convertible	437	6,955				
Super Bee	coupe	7,650		**1972**			
Super Bee	hardtop	18,475	26,125	Charger	coupe	6,370	
GTX	hardtop	14,385		Charger	hardtop	41,717	
GTX	convertible	625	15,010	Charger SE	hardtop	20,266	68,353

Model	Body Style	Total Units	Model Total
Road Runner	hardtop	6,159	
GTX	hardtop	672	6,831
1973			
Charger	coupe	9,788	
Charger	hardtop	41,157	
Charger SE	hardtop	57,026	107,971
Road Runner	hardtop	17,443	17,443
1974			
Charger	coupe	unknown	
Charger	hardtop	24,716	
Charger SE	hardtop	30,957	60,673
Road Runner	hardtop	9,656	9,656

Production By Engine Size

Model Year	Model Name	Engine CI	Total	Percentage of Production
1966	Charger	426 Hemi	468	1.2
1967	Charger	426 Hemi	118	0.07
1967	Coronet R/T*	426 Hemi	283	2.7
1967	GTX*	426 Hemi	720	5.9
1968	Charger R/T	426 Hemi	467	2.6
1968	Coronet R/T			
	hardtop	426 Hemi	220	2.2
	convertible	426 Hemi	9	1.5
1968	Super Bee	426 Hemi	125	1.5
1968	GT hardtop	426 Hemi	410	2.3
	convertible	426 Hemi	36	3.5
1968	Road Runner*	426 Hemi	1,019	2.2
1969	Charger	225 6-cyl	542	0.08
	Charger R/T	426 Hemi	232	1.2
	Charger 500	426 Hemi	52#	11.5
	Daytona	426 Hemi	70	13.9
1969	Coronet R/T			
	hardtop	426 Hemi	232	3.5
	convertible	426 Hemi	101	1.8
1969	Super Bee coupe	426 Hemi	166	2.1
	hardtop	426 Hemi	92	0.04
	hardtop	440 3x2bl	1,010	5.5
	coupe	440 3x2bl	618	8.0
1969	GTX hardtop	426 Hemi	198	1.3
	convertible	426 Hemi	11	1.7
1969	Road Runner			
	coupe	426 Hemi	356	1.0
	hardtop	426 Hemi	422	0.09
	convertible	426 Hemi	10	0.04
	coupe	440 3x2bl	615	1.9
	hardtop	440 3x2bl	797	1.7
1970	Charger	225 6-cyl	221	2.2
	Charger R/T	426 Hemi	112	1.1
	Charger R/T	440 3x2bl	116	1.2

Model Year	Model Name	Engine CI	Total	Percentage of Production
1970	Coronet R/T			
	hardtop	426 Hemi	13	0.05
	convertible	426 Hemi	1	0.04
	hardtop	440 3x2bl	194	8.9
	convertible	440 3x2bl	16	6.7
1970	Super Bee coupe	426 Hemi	4	0.01
	hardtop	426 Hemi	32	0.03
	coupe	440 3x2bl	196	5.3
	hardtop	440 3x2bl	1,072	10.0
1970	GTX hardtop	426 Hemi	72	0.09
	hardtop	440 3x2bl	678	9.4
1970	Road Runner			
	coupe	426 Hemi	74	0.05
	hardtop	426 Hemi	75	0.03
	convertible	426 Hemi	3	0.04
	Super Bird	426 Hemi	135	6.9
	coupe	440 3x2bl	651	4.4
	hardtop	440 3x2bl	1,846	8.8
	convertible	440 3x2bl	34	4.9
	Super Bird	440 3x2bl	716	37.0
1971	Charger coupe	225 6-cyl	221	24.6
	hardtop	225 6-cyl	1,441	3.4
	Charger R/T	426 Hemi	63	2.3
	Super Bee	426 Hemi	22	0.05
	Charger R/T	440 3x2bl	178	6.6
	Super Bee	440 3x2bl	99	2.3
1971	Road Runner	426 Hemi	55	0.04
	Road Runner	440 3x2bl	246	1.8
1971	GTX	426 Hemi	30	1.1
	GTX	440 3x2bl	135	5.1
1972	Charger	440 3x2bl	2#	0.002
1972	Road Runner	440 3x2bl	1#	0.01
Total Hemi Production			6,671	0.07
Total 440 3x2bl			10,904	1.1

* All body styles combined
# Known to exist

1975-1979 B-Body Production Totals

Model Year	Model	Total	Package Option Totals
1975	Charger SE	30,812	No package offered
1975	Road Runner	7,183	No package offered
1976	Charger Coupe	6,613	No package offered
1976	Charger Hdtop.	10,811	No package offered
1976	Charger SE	35,337	6,114 Daytona
1977	Charger SE	36,204	5,225 Daytona
1978	Charger SE	2,735	No package offered
1978	Magnum XE	47,827	861 GTs
1979	Magnum XE	25,367	1,670
1979	Cordoba	73,195	3,811 300s

1973-74 Charger Accent Stripes

Stripe Type/Color	Sales Code	Model Usage
Hood (black)	V21	Optional Rallye Only
Bodyside (brown*)	V6K	Standard Spring Special
Bodyside (red*)	V6R	Optional All
Bodyside (gold*)	V6Y	Optional All
Bodyside (Black)	V6X	Standard Rallye
Upper Body (Blue)	V7B	Standard SE and Hardtop
		Optional Coupe
Upper Body (Green)	V7G	Standard SE and Hardtop
		Optional Coupe
Upper Body (Parchment)	V7L	Standard SE and Hardtop
		Optional Coupe
Upper Body (White)	V7W	Standard SE and Hardtop

Stripe Type/Color	Sales Code	Model Usage
		Optional Coupe
Upper Body (Black)	V7X	Standard SE and Hardtop
		Optional Coupe
Upper Body (Gold)	V7Y	Standard SE and Hardtop
		Optional Coupe
Rear Deck (Black) Double Pinstripe	V8X	Optional All
Bodyside (White)	V9W	Optional Hardtop only

All colors are solid unless marked with an * then are in gradated tones

V9W replaces V7 stripes on Charger Hardtop models.

V9W or V7 codes not used on Charger with Rallye package

Index